Feminism and Theatre

SUE-ELLEN CASE

Reissued Edition

with a Foreword by Elaine Aston

palgrave
macmillan

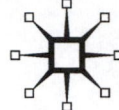

First edition 1988
Reissued edition 2008

Published by PALGRAVE MACMILLAN
Houndmills, Basingstoke, Hampshire RG21 6XS and
175 Fifth Avenue, New York, N.Y. 10010
Companies and representatives throughout the world

PALGRAVE MACMILLAN is the global academic imprint of the
Palgrave Macmillan division of St. Martin's Press, LLC and of Palgrave
Macmillan Ltd. Macmillan® is a registered trademark in the United
States, United Kingdom and other countries. Palgrave is a registered
trademark in the European Union and other countries.

ISBN-13: 978–0–230–52117–9 hardback
ISBN-10: 0–230–52117–7   hardback
ISBN-13: 978–0–230–52118–6 paperback
ISBN-10: 0–230–52118–5   paperback

This book is printed on paper suitable for recycling and made
from fully managed and sustained forest sources. Logging, pulping
and manufacturing processes are expected to conform to the
environmental regulations of the country of origin.

A catalogue record for this book is available from the British Library.

A catalog record for this book is available from the Library of Congress.

10   9   8   7   6   5   4   3   2   1
17 16 15 14 13 12 11 10 09 08

Printed and bound in Great Britain by
Antony Rowe Ltd, Chippenham and Eastbourne

To my parents, Frank Leslie and Flora Gregory Case

Contents

Foreword

Elaine Aston

Forgetting history acts as both a sign and a symptom of a contemporary postmodernity. In this age of forgetting, the reissuing of Sue-Ellen Case's *Feminism and Theatre* serves as a timely reminder that histories are vital to futures. Written at a time when feminism still had a public presence and profile as a social movement, and was a vibrant force in many academic fields of study, *Feminism and Theatre* now (re)appears in a 'postfeminist' moment less certain than the feminist-political 'past'. To forget those histories foundational to the interdisciplinary field of feminism and theatre scholarship and performance practice, however, would be to lose a sense of the critical, creative and collective labour that has gone into thinking, seeing and performing a feminist 'subject' and to lose sight of the future possibilities that this subject may have to offer feminism *and* theatre.

Feminism and theatre: 'new directions'

Case's study was the first of its kind to pay attention to the 'new directions' (to quote the title of the book series in which *Feminism and Theatre* first appeared) that feminism might bring to the theatre academy and to the professional stage, while Case herself has since come to prominence as an important scholar of feminism, theatre and performance theory. Earlier 'feminist theatre' studies had focused on the 1970s emergence of women playwrights and practitioners – for example, Dinah Louise Leavitt's *Feminist Theatre Groups* (1980); Helen Krich Chinoy and Linda Walsh Jenkins's *Women in American Theatre* (1981); or Helene Keyssar's *Feminist Theatre* (1984). Studies of this kind were instrumental in making feminist and/or women's theatre work visible but, to develop this, what was needed – and what Case's study offered – was a more fully rehearsed critical response; critical frameworks appropriate for feminist analysis and 'looking'. As the late Lynda Hart commented in her review of *Feminism and Theatre*, Case's monograph was 'the most intellectually ambitious, politically radical, and theoretically sophisticated book in the field to date'.[1] Moreover, what also made *Feminism and Theatre* distinctive within this beginning field of feminist enquiry was the way in which it sought always to bring discussion and analysis back to the performance context.[2] 'Reading within the text', as Case observed in her opening chapter, as she commented on feminist studies of Shakespeare, is quite a different matter from '[reading] within the practice' (Case, 25). This is an approach she shared with Jill Dolan, whose *Feminist Spectator as Critic* appeared immediately after *Feminism and Theatre*, influenced and inspired by Case.[3] As they mapped out the 'new directions' for feminism in theatre, both publications evidenced a break with theatre's more literary- or dramatic-orientated past and prefigured the theory-practice future.[4]

The attention to practice that Case exemplified is significant in understanding why it was that feminism should begin to make itself felt in theatre studies in the mid- to late 1980s, rather than earlier. As a creative arts subject, theatre is a relatively young discipline – one that has had to struggle for its own autonomy; to get out from under larger, more established disciplines (mostly English Studies), in order to consolidate its core pedagogic components as history, theory and *practice*. There is, then, something of a time lag between feminism as a social movement making its impact in its second wave manifestation in the 1970s, and its coming to have an impact on theatre studies in the 1980s: the struggle for the 'disciplinary rights' to practice meant that 'women's rights' were slower to take effect. This accounts for why, in seeking to elucidate feminist frameworks within theatre studies, Case 'borrowed' from much earlier publications that either came out of feminism as a social movement or came from other disciplines: Kate Millett's *Sexual Politics* (1970) on tackling misogynist images of women; Judith Fetterly's *The Resisting Reader* (1978) on reading against traditional encodings of gender in fiction; Gayle Rubin's highly influential essay for its analysis of the 'traffic in women' (1975), or Laura Mulvey's equally seminal writing on the 'male gaze' in cinema (1975), and so on. In brief, working with hardly any feminist theatre precedents or modes of analysis to draw on, Case was inventing, pioneering a way forward for feminism and theatre studies.

Finding alternatives

If feminism 'begins' anywhere, it begins with feelings of exclusion: with the growing awareness that women's social and cultural lives and activities have been overlooked, marginalised and trivialised by male-dominated social systems and cultural values. It was this sense of exclusion that for feminist scholars working in theatre studies back in the 1980s fuelled the desire to see women's theatre and performance included, rather than excluded, from the theatre syllabus. To be included rather than excluded made it necessary, as Case demonstrated, to revisit the 'traditional history' of the stage; to challenge the patriarchal values of the canonical, the classical in order to make a place, a 'space of our own'. Case went as far as to suggest that for feminist practitioners and scholars, perhaps 'such plays [classics] do not belong in the canon'; that they might not be 'central to the study and practice of theatre' (Case, 19). To challenge the canon in this way was a radical, and for some, outrageous, suggestion – even among feminist scholars who mostly still preferred, for example, to look for the feminism in Shakespeare, rather than countenance the idea that perhaps the bard should not be there at all. Yet to make that challenge was core to recovering the 'losts' and the 'firsts', the women theatre makers that the canonical had 'hidden from history', and to make it possible to chart a counter-cultural, 'alternative' tradition. On the one hand, this meant discovering that women had indeed been writing plays – might even, like Aphra Behn, have struggled to earn a living as a professional writer. On the other hand, Case showed that this also meant learning to look in 'other' places, away from the 'legitimate' stage – in public streets and private dwellings. Out in the margins of 'malestream' theatre, women's 'writing' for performance was often 'other' than, or different from, a playwriting tradition, was 'written' out of bodies that danced, sang or entertained through some kind, any kind, of popular rather than 'high culture' tradition of textual privilege.

Moreover, as Case reflected in the opening to her third chapter, on 'Personal Theatre', it was women's restricted access to the public sphere that accounted for evidence of them performing in domestic spaces, in their homes rather than in theatres. This recognition enabled her to make connections between the salon activities of women from earlier times and the ways in which women began to draw on their personal, domestic lives as a source for feminist performance art in the 1970s. Performing the 'personal as political', which was core to second-wave feminism, women performance artists began to stage a coming-to-political-consciousness of domestic, reproductive and gender oppressions. Including examples of performance-art shows by Carolee Schneeman and Rachel Rosenthal, among others, Case also argued for an idea of 'feminism and theatre' as being more expansive and inclusive than the more conventionally restricted focus on plays and playwrights. While Case's attention to women's performance outside of theatre was important to establishing that women had an 'alternative tradition to the standard history of men in theatre' (Case, 61), it also crucially signalled the desire for a feminist aesthetics: one that would relieve 'women' from their pre-scripted, objectified, traditional gender roles.

Feminisms and aesthetics

The quest for a feminist aesthetics is where feminism and theatre joined forces; is where different feminist positions as political standpoints formed the basis for theatre-making and writing. Feminism as feminisms offered three key positions. Critic and playwright Michelene Wandor (a pioneering figure in feminist theatre in the UK) defined these as bourgeois, radical and socialist. Briefly, these corresponded to: an idea of women being equal to men (bourgeois); giving priority to women's experiences over men's (radical); and, influenced by Marx, paying attention to matters of class and history as well as gender (socialist).[5] US feminists also acknowledged these three positions, though more often referring to them as liberal, radical or cultural, and materialist; and, like Wandor, used them as a critical framework through which to analyse feminist theatres.[6] For feminist practitioners and companies it was not unusual to be explicit about exactly what kind of feminism they identified with. Each feminist political position generated its own recognisable 'tradition' of feminist theatre-making and writing: putting more women centre stage, but within relatively conventional dramatic forms (bourgeois/ liberal); 'writing' out of the body in 'alternative' styles of practice (radical/cultural); and presentational writing and performance techniques that owed much to a Brechtian tradition (socialist/ materialist).

For Case, only radical and materialist feminisms warranted substantial treatment, a reflection arguably of both her lesbian-identified and materialist feminist positions, much as she was otherwise at pains to be even-handed in setting out the directions for feminism and theatre. Instead, she elected for a different 'trilogy' and, importantly, consolidated her attention to radical and materialist feminisms with an examination of 'women of colour and theatre' (Chapter 6). That chapter, more than any other, captures the feminist mood of the 1980s: the moment when feminism had to think self-reflexively about its own (white) agenda. Just as feminism had challenged the patriarchal values that had written women out, and off, in the past, it now had to scrutinise its own shortcomings – specifically its failure adequately to address the complex intersections of race, class and sexuality, a failure that risked 'top girl' hierarchies of privilege. Writing sensitively and tentatively as a white author on black women's politics and theatre, Case signalled what remains a difficult balancing act: the desire to make visible the work by such communities, without colonising, 'owning', or speaking for them.

'Towards a New Poetics'

If the study of 'women of colour and theatre' captured the feminist mood of the 1980s, *Feminism and Theatre's* final chapter, 'Towards a New Poetics', marked the theory explosion of that decade. By this time, theatre studies, along with many other academic disciplines (in the arts and humanities in particular), was being transformed by theoretical models of enquiry; and was open to and opened up by new ways of seeing as it connected and intersected with a diverse body of critical theory. Semiotics, understanding theatre as a complex sign system, shifted critical attention towards how meaning is created and produced. Reception theory brought a consideration of the audience into the meaning-making apparatus, while psychoanalytical theories, applied to theatre contexts, began to examine subject formation and representation. Countering the trend in Women's Studies towards the empirical and the sociological, and reaching out to the feminist theory lodged in English Studies and other disciplines, Case pioneered her own feminist-theory-theatre project. Writing in an accessible, jargon-free way, she brought feminism and theory together to explore what is critically at stake for the female gender to take up the position of subject on the (feminist) stage. The misogynistic attitudes towards women in Aristotle's *Poetics*, explained by Case in her first chapter, suggested the departure point for this 'new poetics': to 'deconstruct the traditional systems of representation and perception of women and posit women in the position of the subject' (Case, 115). Theorisations of 'writing' out of the body or the idea of an *écriture feminine* that came from the philosophical and psychoanalytical thinking of French feminism (Cixous, Irigaray, Kristeva), joined with feminist appropriations of semiotics in the interests of liberating 'women' from the sign of 'Woman'. Despite what for some feminists were argued as the essentialist drawbacks to this kind of feminine morphology, it was an exciting moment of feminist theorising and performance practice. To be 'other' than 'Woman' was widely rehearsed and produced, both on the stage and the critical page.

'Beyond gender'

Case's final chapter, and the idea of a 'new poetics', is one that would preface or open up a whole new chapter for the 'subject' of feminism and theatre. A number of feminist collections on theory and theatre followed in quick succession, among them: Lynda Hart's *Making a Spectacle* (1989); Case's own *Performing Feminisms* (1990); Lynda Hart and Peggy Phelan's *Acting Out: Feminist Performances* (1993), and Helene Keyssar's *Feminist Theatre and Theory* (1996).

The 1990s was also the decade in which feminist thinking joined with gender and queer theorising to consolidate what might best be described as the anti-essentialist, 'beyond gender' project. Departing from the French-influenced philosophies of a feminist 'feminine' body, Judith Butler (*Gender Trouble*, 1990; *Bodies that Matter*, 1993) and others generated lively critical

discussions, philosophical and theoretical debates, and specula-
tions on gender and performativity, in which the citational 'play'
of gender was viewed as an important theoretical paradigm for
positing the release of the subject from the regulations and
constraints of en-gendered (hetero)normativity. Exciting and
stimulating though the 'beyond gender' project generally was, it
also posed the feminism *and* theatre project with some specific
issues – crucially on the issue of agency. Briefly, Butler's discursive theory of performativity moved away from feminism's erstwhile investment in identity politics and 'women' as a category,
towards the critical promise of a subject de-regulated rather than
regulated by oppressive gender norms. However, as Case
observed in her mid-1990s monograph, *The Domain-Matrix*,
where 'Butler gives over . . . agency to a "reiterated acting that is
power in its persistence and instability . . . a nexus of power and
discourse that repeats or mimes the discursive gestures of power"'
this 'contradict[s] traditional agitprop or Brechtian theatrical
strategies that encourage actors and spectators alike to imagine
themselves as an agent of change'.[7] Influenced by Brechtian
strategies and the idea of a social subject (rather than character),
while materialist-feminist theatre practice could not move beyond
or outside the regulating constraints of gender (re-)production, it
could powerfully *demonstrate* oppressive gender norms in the
interests of agency and change. As feminist theorist and theatre
scholar Elin Diamond argued 'When gender is "alienated" or
foregrounded, the spectator is able to see what s/he can't see: a
sign system *as* a sign system' and 'the payoffs, especially where
gender is concerned, can be stunning'.[8] In consequence, as much
as feminist theatre scholarship in the 1990s was stirred up and
excited by the gender thinking of Butler and others, it also sought
to argue the importance of theatre's own feminist theoretical
project of *doing* gender resistant work; of arguing theatre's own
ability to *make* 'gender trouble'.

At the same time, it shared in the contestation of 'women' as
category, looking not just to the alienation of gender, but also to
the intersections of gender with issues of sexuality, race and class.
In particular, as Case first signalled in her seminal discussion of
women of colour and theatre, there was every need for feminism
to think outside its site of (white) Western privilege. In the 1990s,
in response to overcoming or undoing the hierarchical (colonialist)

arrangement of 'First' and 'Third' World, *international* feminism, and influenced by postcolonial theorists such as Gayatri Spivak, there was a move towards transnational feminism: a more demo-cratic, progressive model of cross-border thinking. This had an impact on feminist theatre scholarship which attended to Diasporic subjectivities, representations and aesthetics at 'home', as well as to local feminist performance practices and theatre within the global arena.[9] Moving 'beyond gender' the critical concern and theoretical theatre project was to consider a complex array of identities (of nation, class, race, gender, sexuality) for their contestations and destabilisations of traditional, theatrical systems of representation.

'Feminist residue'

In retrospect it is perhaps not surprising to find a coincidence between the move into 'pure' (gender) theory and the decline of feminism as a political movement. Without the grassroots activism, the feminism of the streets and protests that took place *outside* of the academy augured a possible separation between theory and practice; between a world of philosophical ideas and social realities. Any project that set out today to offer an equiva-lent undertaking to Case's 1988 study would almost certainly need to map this gender theory project, as much as it would need to situate a consideration of theatre and performance within a contemporary 'postfeminist' climate and culture. There is no getting away from the fact that feminism can no longer lay claim to and benefit from a political movement forging communities of women who share a commitment to social and political change. Nor, in the theatre, is it possible to find a feminist network of companies and practitioners consolidating a body of work that is easily identifiable and visible as 'feminist theatre', given the disappearance and disbanding of those kinds of feminist theatre communities in the early 1990s.[10] On the other hand, it is possi-ble to trace what Janelle Reinelt, whose theatre scholarship yields important transatlantic analyses of feminism and theatre, refers to as a 'feminist residue' in contemporary theatre: 'serious issues [that] have been identified and are still present', even though these are more often 'ignored, pushed aside or simply denied'.[11] Looking to these serious, residual issues, it is possible to come to a critical understanding of the ways in which feminist views remain important in theatre and to the material conditions of theatrical production.

'Women' playwrights

Mirroring the 'beyond gender' spirit of the 1990s, 'women' playwrights were increasingly anxious to contest the gender categorisation of their work. This represented a significant departure from the 1970s identification of theatre as feminist or woman-centred. This is not, however, to be confused with the idea that an established, feminist generation of playwrights, such as the UK's Caryl Churchill, Timberlake Wertenbaker, Sarah Daniels and Bryony Lavery, or a younger generations of writers, such as Phyllis Nagy, Rebecca Prichard or Judy Upton, were moving away from feminism, or even joining the anti-feminist backlash. On the contrary, any analysis of theatre by these writers reveals an enduring commitment to the 'residual' matters of women's social and cultural exclusion. In the 1990s, for example, Daniels dramatised work for theatre and radio that dealt variously with domestic and child abuse (*Beside Herself*, 1990; *The Madness of Esme and Shaz*, 1994) and postnatal depression (*Purple Side Coasters*, 1995), while Wertenbaker tackled infertility as a feminist issue (*The Break of Day*, 1995), and Lavery staged lesbian romance (*Her Aching Heart*, 1990).

What was resisted, however, was that this socially and politically aware theatre-making should be 'seen', categorised and ghettoised by the 'woman' label. Butler's contestation of gender norms resonates in many of the observations and comments made by (women) writers on this issue: 'Categories are a curse' (Clare McIntyre);[12] 'the label constructs an identity for the writer which excludes a kind of complexity of interpretation' (Winsome Pinnock);[13] 'I have no responsibility as a woman writer because I don't believe there's such a thing' (Sarah Kane).[14] Writing 'beyond' gender categorisation, dramatic worlds were no longer defined and confined by women's issues, but connected to a much larger, social, cultural and political canvas. That canvas was also responsive to dramatising a contemporary world in which both socialist and feminist agendas were diminished and displaced. Given the climate of social and political disenchantment and disenfranchisement, this in turn invited theatrical interrogation of social agency and change.

At the same time, 'new' labels came into play. In British theatre, for example, the 1990s was labelled as the decade of the 'young', the 'angry' and the *'male'*.[15] The critical focus on all-things-masculine meant, paradoxically, that 'women' had to fight to hang on to the cultural ground gained by the earlier, feminist challenge to the sexual politics of theatre: the gender hierarchies that keep more men than women in positions of power. There was a similar gender imbalance in the USA. Reinelt, for example, quotes some depressing statistics that evidence the relative paucity of women in the position of directors and as writers for the American stage.[16] In brief, 'women' writers and practitioners still found that gender 'mattered' when it came to the commissioning and production process. Even with years of substantial writing experience, it was not uncommon to be treated as 'emergent' or in need of 'development'.[17] Once staged, there was the additional and enduring difficulty of having work seen and reviewed by critics – still largely male, white, middle-class and not adverse to 'boxing' women back into a 'sub'-gender category.

Live art and performance art

This inability to overcome completely the sexual inequalities of the theatre profession, and the more general difficulties that writers of either gender face in making theatre 'pay', has a bearing on the 1990s explosion of live art and performance art practice, and the rise of the female solo artist – now a more significant figure than the erstwhile 1970s paradigm of the feminist group or collective. Published in 1990, Lenora Champagne's *Out From Under* brought together scripts by US women performance artists, including Karen Finley, Holly Hughes, Rachel Rosenthal and Fiona Templeton.[18] In the UK, successful solos have been staged by performance artists Bobby Baker, Marisa Carnesky, Kazuko Hohki and Helen Paris, among others. These alternative-to-theatre traditions are also where women artists from ethnically diverse communities on both sides of the Atlantic have found the 'space' in which to perform race- and gender-aware work: Anna Deavere Smith, Coco Fusco, Robbie McCauley, Vayu Naidu and SuAndi. In brief, if written today, Case's 'personal theatre' paradigm would have a substantial legacy to add to that of earlier feminist performance, and to the attraction performance holds for artists in 'scripting' (out of) themselves, rather then being 'authored' by someone else's text. It would also have a significant 'body' of critical theoretical work to survey, examining ideas of the body as text and analysing the importance of feminist autobiographical strategies in performance.[19]

Moreover, a renewed consideration of performance art would also be looking to the way in which body artistry has continued and consolidated a lively and controversial feminist tradition – from Carolee Schneeman's scroll pulled out from her vagina in the 1970s (*Interior Scroll*), to the in-yer-face Karen Finley and porn star Annie Sprinkle in the 1980s and 1990s. Sprinkle has also been an important role model for younger generations of women artists involved in today's US 'new burlesque' scene (especially popular in New York). Hypersexualising burlesque, this appropriation of a popular tradition by women artists reflects the new self-/sexual confidence of younger generations of women. And, finally, no feminist discussion of contemporary body art would be complete without some reference to the controversial French artist Orlan and her radical, interventionist cosmetic body surgery.[20]

'Performing elsewhere'

One of the characteristics of live art and performance art traditions has been the idea of 'performing elsewhere': of occupying non-theatre spaces as well as theatre venues. As Leslie Hill (of Curious) writes, '[s]ome contemporary performance is "housed" within the familiar architecture of a theatre or gallery, while some work is "homeless" setting up temporary camp'.[21] In the 1970s feminist companies often 'housed' their shows in small-scale theatre studios, alongside the 'temporary camps' of church halls, community centres, private homes or any kinds of spaces in which women could come together as a community. Similarly, today, Bobby Baker appears in studio theatres as well as in her kitchen, local school, community centre or church.[22] Performing in a domestic or community space, while not exclusive to a *women's* performance tradition, constitutes a significant 'feminist residue' in the potential that these other sites continue to offer for politicising 'daily life'.

By contrast, the advances made in technology since the writing of *Feminism and Theatre* have created a different kind of 'performing elsewhere': of performing in cyberspace. If street theatre in the 1970s was where women staged embodied protests against dominant cultures of femininity, their protests over the 'Miss World' contests, for example, today's feminist activism finds a disembodied 'place' on the web. A prime example is the 'Guerilla Performance Locator' by Curious.[23] Invoking a tradition of performance art that links today's political activists back to the suffragettes, the 'Locator' invites activists worldwide to make spectacles of themselves and to map their work on the site. The advantage of the web is that it provides a relatively inexpensive 'place' in which to make a political performance intervention into 'homes' across the globe (or to those parts of the globe that are privileged by technology). This activist appropriation of technology suggests the web as a new, electronic kind of (global) street theatre.

Feminism and theatre – the future

As much as this brief survey of a 'feminist residue' in theatre and performance argues some important feminist attachments, feminism's future is dependent on its ability to play an effective and affective part in women's social and cultural lives. In particular, feminism must find and define an 'audience' or community of younger generations of women.

Feminism's appeal, however, is somewhat limited when it comes to younger generations, who more often perceive feminism as being outmoded and redundant, and not important to their lives: feminism is not something with which they necessarily wish to identify. 'Many of my young women students often show interest in women's studies or gender issues while simultaneously insisting with strong conviction they are NOT feminists' observes Reinelt.[24] 'How ... can this [feminism] be a word that strikes such terror in the hearts of young women today, so hasty to have it known that they are NOT feminists?' ask 'curious feminists', Hill and Paris.[25] Perhaps the answer is, on the one hand, the 'terror' that the popular media image of the feminist as a bra-burning women's-libber of the 1970s strikes, and, on the other, the legacy and appeal of the new style of sexualised, non-politicised, girl-power 'feminism' of the 1990s.

Despite all this, there are connections that can be made to feminism through the theatre classroom and workshop – not as an object of historical study, but as a subject that is relevant to and renewable in the present moment. To make this happen requires a cross-generational negotiation between those of us who grew up with feminism, and students studying and practising theatre today. One pedagogic strategy is to make contemporary theatre and performance histories meaningful and relevant to the next generation of makers and scholars. Dolan, for example, organised an institutional project at the University of Austin, Texas, in which she brought together performances by a feminist generation of solo women artists to perform for, discuss and work with her students.[26] What she was keen to achieve by doing this was to communicate her 'own urgent sense of feminist performance history' and to establish that, 'as a new generation of performance artists takes hold, we honor women whose work in many ways founded the genre'.[27] Just as Case identified the important 'firsts' for women in theatre and performance histories, in the current moment, when it is all too easy for women to lose the social and cultural advantages fought for by an earlier generation, it is vital that students understand and engage with their contemporary feminist performance heritage in order to 'make' their own feminist (performance) futures.

Also significant in Dolan's case study is the way that the cross-generational debate involves the feminist artists themselves. Seeing the artists, hearing them tell their performance histories, stories and politics is a means of communicating the passion and commitment that goes into 'making' feminist/m work. It creates the opportunity to *move* young women to thinking and talking about feminism; to make feminism come 'alive' as a point of political identification. Beyond the influence and inspiration this affords a new generation of practitioners and scholars, it also suggests a way of making new contacts, communities and networks. In the UK, the 'Women's Writing for Performance Project', which had an institutional base in Lancaster University, has achieved just that, by setting up a funded workshop programme of high-profile women artists, who shared their skills, processes and performance stories with emergent practitioners, with scholars and other artists.[28]

Reviewing *Feminism and Theatre* in 1989, Hart summed up the monograph as 'call for participation'; an invitation to others to pursue, and to open up the 'groundwork' Case had laid down.[29] Despite these less auspicious feminist times, the reissuing of *Feminism and Theatre* in 2008 renews that 'call for participation'. Indeed, there are some hopeful signs that feminist theatre and performance scholarship is again gathering momentum. In 2007, Palgrave Macmillan also published *Staging Black Feminisms* (Lynette Goddard); *Women in Irish Drama* (Melissa Sihra); *Staging International Feminisms* (edited by Elaine Aston and Sue-Ellen Case), and *Performance Practice and Process: Contemporary [Women] Practitioners* (Elaine Aston and Geraldine Harris). Situated alongside this body of new work, the cartography of feminism and theatre that Case mapped in 1988, a 'first' in its own right, is a seminal and inspirational source for looking back and for inviting future, hopefully feminist, generations of theatre students, scholars and practitioners to participate in the field of feminism and theatre which she was so instrumental in and vital to pioneering.

Notes

1. Lynda Hart, *Theatre Journal*, 41.2 (May 1989), p. 263.
2. With an 'approach ... tied to performance', wrote another reviewer, '*Feminism and Theatre* will help teachers, directors, actors and young playwrights', Rosette C. Lamont, *Modern Drama*, 32.1 (1989), p. 159.
3. As a graduate student, Dolan took a class with Case at NYU, and acknowledges her debt to Case as 'an invaluable role model'; as someone who 'has blazed the trail for feminist theatre critics in the academy and in the profession', *The Feminist Spectator as Critic* (Ann Arbor, Mich.: University of Michigan Press, 1988), p. xi.
4. For a comparative, joint review of both publications, see Judith Pipper, *Theatre Research International*, 15.1 (1989), pp. 95–8.
5. See Michelene Wandor, *Carry On Understudies: Theatre and Sexual Politics* (London: Routledge, 1986), ch. 8, 'Political Dynamics: The Feminisms', pp. 130–9. This was an important addition to Wandor's original publication, *Understudies* (1981).
6. For helpful examples and further explanation, see Dolan *The Feminist Spectator as Critic*, ch. 1, 'The Discourse of Feminisms', pp. 1–18; and Gayle Austin, *Feminist Theories for Dramatic Criticism* (Ann Arbor, Mich.: University of Michigan Press, 1990), pp. 4–6.
7. Sue-Ellen Case, *The Domain-Matrix* (Bloomington and Indianapolis, Ind.: Indiana University Press, 1996), p. 15.
8. Elin Diamond, *Unmaking Mimesis* (London: Routledge, 1997), p. 47.

9. For more on this topic, see the special edition of *Theatre Research International*, 24.3 (1999) ed. by Sue-Ellen Case and Jung-Soon Shim.

10. On the life, times and demise of feminist theatre groups, see Charlotte Canning's *Feminist Theaters in the USA* (London: Routledge, 1996), and, for the British context, Elaine Aston (ed.), *Feminist Theatre Voices* (Loughborough: Loughborough Theatre Texts, 1999).

11. Janelle Reinelt, 'Navigating Postfeminism: Writing Out of the Box', in Elaine Aston and Geraldine Harris (eds), *Feminist Futures? Theatre, Performance, Theory* (Basingstoke: Palgrave Macmillan, 2006), p. 20.

12. Clare McIntyre, 'Plays by Women' in David Edgar (ed.), *State of Play* (London: Faber, 1999), pp. 56–7.

13. Pinnock, in Edgar, *State of Play*, p. 58.

14. Sarah Kane Interview, in Heidi Stephenson and Natasha Langridge (eds), *Rage and Reason: Women Playwrights on Playwriting* (London: Methuen, 1997), p. 134.

15. For discussion of theatre and masculinities in the 1990s, see David Edgar's 'Provocative Acts: British Playwriting in the Post-war Era and Beyond', in Edgar (ed.), *State of Play*, pp. 3–34; and in the same volume, Mark Ravenhill's 'Plays About Men', pp. 48–55.

16. See Reinelt, 'Navigating Postfeminism', p. 21.

17. For more on this issue, see Asian-British playwright Tanika Gupta's comments in Stephenson and Langridge (eds), *Rage and Reason*, p. 116; and performance artist Fiona Templeton's comments in 'Angry Again? – New York Women Artists and Feminists Futures', in Aston and Harris (eds), *Feminist Futures*, p. 218.

18. Lenora Champagne (ed.) *Out From Under: Texts by Women Performance Artists* (New York: Theatre Communications Group, 1990).

19. For examples, see Amelia Jones and Andrew Stephenson (eds), *Performing the Body/Performing the Text* (London: Routledge, 1999); Sidonie Smith and Julia Watson (eds), *Interfaces: Women, Autobiography, Image, Performance* (Ann Arbor, Mich.: University of Michigan Press, 2002); and Maggie Gale and Viv Varner (eds), *Auto/biography and Identity* (Manchester: Manchester University Press, 2004).

20. For information, visit http://www.orlan.net/.

21. In Leslie Hill and Helen Paris (eds), *Performance and Place* (Basingstoke: Palgrave Macmillan 2006), p. xiii.

22. For details, visit http://www.bobbybakersdailylife.com/.

23. Visit http://www.placelessness.com/guerilla/index.htm.

24. Reinelt, 'Navigating Postfeminism', p. 20.

25. Leslie Hill and Helen Paris, ' Curious Feminists', in Aston and Harris (eds), *Feminist Futures?*, p. 57.

26. See Dolan, 'Performance, Utopia, and the "Utopian Performative"', *Theatre Journal*, 53 (2001), 455–79. The artists in question were Holly Hughes, Peggy Shaw and Deb Margolin.

27. Ibid, p. 464.

28. For details, visit http://www.lancs.ac.uk/depts/theatre/womenwriting/.

29. Hart, *Theatre Journal*, p. 263.

Acknowledgements

The reissue of this book has prompted a revision of my acknowledgements.

First, I am still working in the tradition of reading feminist theory and criticism that I learned from the members of the Feminist Colloquium at the University of Washington – especially the expertise of Sydney Kaplan, Yvonne Yarbro-Bejarano and Carolyn Allen. Also, my PhD students there, Katrin Sieg, Juli Thompson-Burk. Charlotte Canning and Jeanie Forte, brought inspiration and particular expertise to my feminist project.

Since the first publication of the book in 1988, the field of feminism and theatre has grown to include seminal texts by Elin Diamond, Jill Dolan, Janelle Reinelt, Diana Taylor, and many, many others who have helped to create this field. A myriad of feminist artists continue to enrich the field, but, for me, particularly, the work of *Split Britches*. Elaine Aston's work has been of such a pioneering and enduring value to the field that I asked her to write the foreword to this volume.

The International Feminist Working Group has expanded my sense of feminist practice in the world, particularly the contributions of Jung-Soon Shim, Tiina Rosenberg, Antje Budde, Elizabeth Sakellaridou, Fawzia Afzal Kahn, and Katherine Mezur. My debt to my earliest mentor, Ruby Cohn, who offered an early example of an independent woman scholar, continues to inform my work. In my personal life, feminist families continue to nurture my ability to continue in the struggle for a recognition of the talented and brilliant work of feminist scholars and practitioners. I am especially grateful to Marian Chapman, who has since passed on, and my life partner, Susan Leigh Foster.

I am grateful to Macmillan, Methuen/Routledge and now Palgrave Macmillan for the willingness to publish texts in this field.

S.-E. C.

Introduction

I have not organised this book along either developmental or chronological lines. Instead, it is organised like a sampler of feminist critical techniques, theories, political positions, issues, explorations and theatre practices. Each chapter and each of its constituent sections is relatively complete in itself, allowing the reader either to read it in the order in which it appears, or to pick out for independent reference a section on a single author, such as Aphra Behn, a single position, such as materialist feminism, or a single theory, such as semiotics. However, in attempting to outline the overall relationship between the feminist movement and work in the theatre, I have built the discussion on three bases: history, practice and theory.

My discussion of the feminist uses of history and theatre begins with a deconstruction of the classics of the canon (Chapter 1). Because I work in the theatre, rather than in literary criticism, I have tied the perspective on the classics to stage practice rather than to a reading of the texts. Also, I have adopted an academic style, since I feel that any feminist deconstruction of the 'masterpieces' is an invitation to the guardians of the tradition to attack its weaknesses with the standards of quill and scroll. I hope these re-visions of the masters can provide an overview of work that has already been done in this area as well as suggest some new ideas and future projects. I debated whether or not to begin this book with works by men, but finally decided that many of us originally adopted feminism because of the pain and anger we felt when we encountered the prejudices and omissions of the traditional theatre. This deconstruction is only one of many ways for feminists to think their way out of its patriarchal prescriptions.

Chapters 2 and 3 focus exclusively on women's works. I wanted to separate their achievements from those in the canon. I have tried out several new ideas, such as 'personal theatre' (Chapter 3) – not so much for the sake of establishing a new genre as to illustrate a way in which a feminist critic can extend the limits of theatre history by simply considering the experiences of women as definitive. At the same time, I hoped to 'name' a few of the relatively invisible but pioneering women in traditional theatre, so that feminists can claim a heritage (Chapter 2). Finally, I wanted to end the historical section of the book with a consideration of the performances of contemporary women who seem to be on the cutting edge of the art, but whose works resonate with women's voices from the past (Chapter 3).

When I began to write this book, I contacted many feminists in theatre practice and in the academic world, asking them, 'If you saw this book in a bookstore, what would you hope to find in it?' Many of them responded that they wanted to see some guidelines, a sampling of ways to evaluate theatre work from within feminist politics. The chapters on radical and materialist feminisms and women of colour (4–6) were designed to create that connection between the social movement and the stage. These chapters were both exciting and frightening to write – exciting, because I had never seen the project tried before and frightening because of the many political decisions that had to be made while writing. Once again, I did not intend to provide any definitive account, but only to suggest a place to begin, or a way to work. I asked several feminists to read and critique these chapters, particularly the one on women of colour. Nevertheless, I still have many doubts and deficiencies in these areas. I hope the reader will feel that any disagreements she or he may have with the content of these sections are a necessary part of the continuing discovery, debate and dialogue on these issues. Certainly, these chapters are the ones most embedded in my own historical, economic, educational and geographical situation.

The final chapter, on theory (7), participates in the kind of language that feminist theoreticians employ. In fact, I hope that it introduces and explains the language to some extent. In so far as I was able, I avoided jargon and dense constructions and aimed for a clear explanation of the concepts. Again, I included this chapter because of the many debates I have heard over these issues, making them so alive in feminist circles. Yet many people are still confused about where to begin in theory and where to look for the texts. I hope this chapter at least provides a way into the materials. Very little work has been published that relates these theories to a feminist perspective on the theatre. I have borrowed from works on film and on the novel to begin an application of these theories to theatre practice.

I think the backbone of this book lies in the suggested readings and the bibliography. Because most of the work on feminism and theatre is published scattered about a variety of journals and unpublished sources, relating to a variety of disciplines, I have researched a number of different areas, hoping to compile a list of quality materials. This book contains references to the authors and titles most prominent in the field, and the bibliography provides an essential reading-list for an introduction to the overall theme. Moreover, I have chosen to cite works that themselves contain excellent bibliographies. I hope that in the future someone will publish anthologies of secondary materials on feminism and theatre, making articles in out-of-print and limited editions available to a wider audience, as well as creating a sourcebook of feminist criticism in theatre. In so far as any anthologies exist, they focus primarily on plays and playwrights, ignoring practice and critical issues.

Finally, I should like to raise the issue of the authorial voice in this book. I know that many feminists consider the first person ('I') to be the 'politically correct' voice in which to write. I agree with that position to the degree to which it unmasks the invisible author and reveals her gender and her racial and class bias. I think my own white, academic background permeates all of this book. I also admire the way in which feminist authors who use the subjective voice in their work, expose the layers of personal experience, and even draw attention to the subconscious slips in their discourse. As a feminist, I, too, find the subjective voice to be a liberation from the impersonal, omniscient and seemingly objective voice patriarchal culture has used for centuries to render certain experiences invisible and to gain power through the printed word. I, too, hope feminists can discover a new, alternative voice.

I chose not to use the subjective voice for several reasons, but, foremost, because I did not want this book to be an argument for my own political position. Though my historical roots are in radical feminism, I consider myself to be a materialist feminist.

Certainly, a close reading of this book would reveal both its radical and materialist biases. Yet, as much as I may personally disagree with certain political issues, or even certain feminist theatres and performances, I felt it was more important to share what information I had on them than to evaluate them from one single position. While I realise that the voice I employ in this text reifies many of the values of the patriarchy, it seemed precipitious to me to use this opportunity to argue my own beliefs. But, finally, I must also admit that, since my training and practice have been in this 'objective' voice, I do not yet fully comprehend how to combine a personal voice with discussion of such things as historical figures and events. However, I feel it is important at least to raise this issue and admit my own limitations.

This book was written in 1985, when the feminist movement was only twenty years old and feminist theatre practice younger still. Nevertheless, I think it suggests the radical way in which feminism has affected all aspects of theatre, changing theatre history and becoming a major element in twentieth-century theatre practice. The feminist critic or practitioner need no longer adopt a polemic posture in this art, but can rely on the established feminist tradition in the theatre, with its growing number of practitioners and adherents.

Chapter 1

Traditional History:
A Feminist Deconstruction

Classic drag: the male creation of female parts

General principles

From a feminist perspective, initial observations about the history of theatre noted the absence of women within the tradition. Since traditional scholarship has focused on evidence related to written texts, the absence of women playwrights became central to early feminist investigations. The fact that there was no significant number of extant texts written by women for the stage until the seventeenth century produced a rather astounding sense of absence in the classical traditions of the theatre. The silence of women's voices in these traditions led feminist historians who were interested in women playwrights to concentrate on periods in which they did emerge: primarily the seventeenth century in England, the nineteenth century in America and the twentieth century in Europe and America. These studies produced, beginning in the early 1970s, a number of new anthologies of plays by women and biographies of women playwrights.

Work on the classical periods became possible by studying the image of women within plays written by men. Many scholars attribute the beginning of this type of textual discovery to Millett's influential book *Sexual Politics* (1970), which illustrated a way to recognise and interpret the images of women in male literature as misogynistic. *Sexual Politics* offered a way to read against texts by becoming aware of their gendered bias and, as the title suggests, to foreground the notion that art is not distinct from politics. While Millett's book concentrated on describing the images of women, other early works such as Judith Fetterly's *The Resisting Reader* showed how to resist reading texts by men as they were conventionally read. Fetterly outlined ways of reading against texts to discover the feminist subtext latent in such subversions. Works on images of women still predominate in the feminist criticism of classical texts. Numerous revisions of Aeschylus and Shakespeare are currently being published. There are two basic types of image: positive roles, which depict women as independent, intelligent and even heroic; and a surplus of misogynistic roles commonly identified as the Bitch, the Witch, the Vamp and the Virgin/Goddess. These roles reflect the perspective of the playwright or the theatrical tradition on women. Originally, feminist historians used these theatrical images of women as evidence of the kind of lives actual women might have lived in the period – for example, the information the characters and situations of Medea or Phaedra might give us about the lives of powerful women in Greece. This approach was useful because traditional socio-economic histories tend to exhibit the same absence of women as does the literature. In the 1970s, ground-breaking work on women in history was done in both realms: the socio-historical evidence afforded by theatrical texts was identified, and documents on laws, social practices and economic restrictions on women in history were collated and published. This work enabled feminist critics and historians to produce a new kind of cultural analysis, based on the interplay of cultural and socio-economic evidence, to discover the nature of women's lives in the classical periods.

The availability of these materials led to a new understanding of the complicity of art with political projects, as well as the complicity of traditional history with the patriarchy, reversing the original interpretations of these documents. Feminist critics began to perceive that in studying the representation of women in classical plays and histories it was of fundamental importance to distinguish between private and public life. Public life is privileged in these sources, while private life remains relatively invisible. The new feminist analyses prove that this division is gender-specific: i.e. public life is the property of men, and women are relegated to the invisible private sphere. As a result of the suppression of real women, the culture invented its own representation of the gender, and it was this fictional 'Woman' who appeared on stage, in the myths and in the plastic arts, representing the patriarchal values attached to the gender while suppressing the experiences, stories, feelings and fantasies of actual women. (See Teresa de Lauretis for a development of this concept.) The new feminist approach to these cultural fictions distinguishes this 'Woman' as a male-produced fiction from historical women, insisting that there is little connection between the two categories. Within theatre practice, the clearest illustration of this division is in the tradition of the all-male stage. 'Woman' was played by male actors in drag, while real women were banned from the stage. This practice reveals the fictionality of the patriarchy's representation of the gender. Classical plays and theatrical conventions can now be regarded as allies in the project of suppressing real women and replacing them with masks of patriarchal production.

Application

The beginning of the Western tradition of theatre is traditionally dated from the Athenian festivals of Dionysos in the sixth and fifth centuries BC. Our notions of drama, acting, physical theatre space, costume, mask and the relation between actors and audience can be said to stem from these festivals, their rites and ceremonies. In the sixth century, both women and men participated in them, but during the fifth century, when the ceremonies were becoming what is known as theatre, women disappeared from the practice. No record has been found of any law forbidding women to participate in the songs and dances, nor is there any evidence for the precise date of the change. Margarete Bieber, a recognised authority on the Greek and Roman theatre, merely notes that it was 'Attic morality' that 'banished women from public life'.[1] This implies that the reason for the exclusion of women must be sought in the emerging cultural codes of Athens, rather than in specific political or theatrical developments. Three areas of change – in socio-economic organisation, in the creative arts and in the predominant myths – help us to understand the change in theatrical practice. The intersection of all of these elements may be recognised in the text of *The Oresteia*.

Among the new economic practices, the rise of the family unit radically altered the role of women in Greek public life. Ironically, the important role women began to assume within the family unit was the cause of their removal from public life. The family unit became the site for the creation and transmission of personal wealth. With the rise of the *polis* (the city state), the extended network of relationships characteristic of aristocracies gave way to single families as the basis of social organisation. The increased use of metals as commodities and the small-scale cultivation of land made it possible for individuals to control their own wealth. Yet, while ownership became more individual and confined to the family unit, it was largely limited to the male gender. The rights of women to own and exchange property were severely restricted. For example, women could only inherit in the absence of a male and were not allowed to barter for property over one *medimnos* (bushel). Within this new economy, women became a medium of exchange and marriage became an institution of ownership.[2] In fact, the Greek word for marriage, *ekdosis*, meant 'loan' – women were loaned to their husbands by their fathers, and in the case of divorce, were returned to their fathers.

With this change in economic organisation came a concomitant change in political organisation. The *oikos*, or household, became the basis of citizenship.[3] Citizenship was dependent upon family lines – a son was granted citizenship only if his parents were citizens, but without a son the parents could not retain their citizenship. This rule led to the strict definition and regulation of the sex life of the woman. The mother–wife acquired new moral and legal responsibilities in relation to the legitimacy and security of heirs and, by extension, political membership of the *polis*. Clear lines of descent were vital to the *polis*, making adultery a crime against society rather than a matter only of personal transgression. Yet, at the same time as the household became controlled by the needs of the state, its activities became totally separate from those which were considered the business of the state or as belonging to public life. As Nancy Hartsock puts it in her book *Money, Sex and Power*, the Greeks defined the household as a private, apolitical space quite distinct from the public, political space of the *polis*: 'The result was a theorization of politics and political power as activities that occurred in a masculine arena characterized by freedom from necessary labor, dominance of intellect or soul,' while the domestic space was defined by necessary labour and as a place where bodily needs were dominant.[4] Since Athenian women were confined to the house (explicitly, in the laws of Solon), they were removed from the public life of the intellect and the soul, lost their economic and legal powers, and were confined to the world of domestic labour, child-bearing and concomitant sexual duties. Given their exclusion from the public life of the *polis* and their diminished role in its socio-economic organisation, it is not surprising that their participation in the Dionysian festivals became restricted to private observance and that they were duly excluded from the public stage.

Alongside these changes in socio-economic organisation came new cultural institutions – theatre being only one among several. Athens created new architecture, new religions and new myths. These cultural institutions became allied with the suppression of women by creating the new gender role of 'Woman', which served to privilege the masculine gender and oppress the feminine one. At base, the new cultural categories of gender were constructed as categories of difference and polarity.[5] 'Woman' appeared as the opposite of man. This move can best be seen in the new myths and associated architectural depictions of the Amazons, which conflate female gender with the image of the outsider and with characteristics typical of the male. The Amazons, dangerous but defeated, reverse the 'natural' gender roles. They are warriors who force men to do 'women's' work, such as child-rearing, while the women go off to war.[6] The Amazons also embody other myths of gender reversal: for instance, they keep female babies and dispose of male ones, whereas the custom (in Sparta, for instance) was to dispose of female babies.[7] Moreover, the word 'Amazon' (meaning 'no breast') ties such practices to a biological secondary sex characteristic specific to the female. The new architecture of the Acropolis, the civic centre of Athens, displays the downfall of the Amazons and the rise of Athena. Central to the new political order, then, is the fall of these women who would defy correct gender associations and the rise of a woman who would enforce the new image of 'Woman' in the *polis*. This demise of the old images of women and the rise of Athena are central themes in *The Oresteia*.

The genealogy of the gods provides the mytho-historical context for this creation of the new 'Woman'. The history of the gods explains why genders are opposite, locked in conflict, and why the male gender must defeat the female. The myth of the primeval goddess and earth mother Gaia is a story of the dangers of her womb – the story of her children is one of murders and castrations. In the end Zeus is victorious: he swallows his wife, Metis, in order to gain her power of reproduction and then gives birth to Athena. Athena represents the end of the dangers of the womb, for she has no mother (breaking the matriarchal line and subverting identification with her own sex), has no sexuality (she remains a virgin), defeats the Amazons, allies herself with the reign of Zeus and Apollo, and thereby brings order to Athens. At about the same time as Athena rose to prominence, the cult of Dionysos appeared in Athens and usurped from earlier female goddesses their associations with fertility and sexuality, while boys assimilated female sexuality in the social practice of male homosexuality (later idealised by Plato). This male usurpation of female fertility later became a metaphor for philosophical inquiry in Plato's *Theatetus*, where he asserts that his art of midwifery is for 'men, not women, and my concern is not with the body but with the soul', for he deals with 'the offspring of a young man's thought' (lines 150b–c).[8] The genealogy of the gods, in dividing female sexuality from power, presaged the assimilation of female sexuality by Dionysos and the isolation of power in the image of the motherless virgin Athena. In turn, the new mythology also presaged the same usurpation of female fertility in Plato's idealism.

The rise of drama, in the context of the Athenian state festivals dedicated to Dionysos, places theatre securely within this new patriarchal institution of gender wars. Theatre must be gender-specific to the male and enact the suppression of real women and the creation of the new 'Woman'. The maenads (the female celebrants in the Dionysian festivals) must dance into oblivion, while the satyrs (the male celebrants) must become the first choruses of the new drama. 'The singer Arion is said to have given to the singers of the dithyramb . . . the costume of the satyrs. The practice of representing someone other than oneself grew out of this ecstasy and led to the mimic art of the actors.'[9] In other words, the very invention of acting was gender-specific: the actor was the satyr.

The gender-specific quality of the actor in the satyr play was even underscored by his wearing of a leather phallus. Thus, the actor/dramatic subject was male. Yet, for the battle of the genders, the female too had to be represented: a male actor had to perform the female role. Though literary critics and theatre historians tend to mention this strange phenomenon only in passing, Bieber does note one specific problem for male actors in their representation of women: as depicted on vases, the maenads seem to be in a state of ecstasy – to play them the male actors needed to understand the religious emotion felt by these women.[10] Yet a more central problem emerges: how does a man depict a woman? How does the male actor signal to the audience that he is playing a female character? Besides wearing the female costume (with short tunic) and the female mask (with long hair), he might have indicated gender through gesture, movement and intonation. In considering this portrayal, it is important to remember that the notion of the female derived from the male point of view, which remained alien to female experience and reflected the perspective of the gendered opposite. This vocabulary of gestures initiated the image of 'Woman' as she is seen on the stage – institutionalised through patriarchal culture and represented by male-originated signs of her appropriate gender behaviour. Moreover, the practice of male actors playing women probably encouraged the creation of female roles which lent themselves to generalisation and stereotype. The depiction and development of female characters in the written texts must have been accommodated to the way they were presented on stage. Though all characters were formalised and masked, even with cross-gender casting for female characters these were distinguished in kind from the male characters. A subtextual message was delivered about the nature of the female gender, its behaviour, appearance, and formal distance from the representation of the male.

The Athenian theatre practice created a political and aesthetic arena for ritualised and codified gender behaviour, linking it to civic privileges and restrictions. This gender principle was elevated to 'classic' status and so became a paradigmatic element in the history of theatre, connoting the expulsion of women from the canon and the ideal. The etymology of 'classic', connoting 'class', indicates that this expulsion is also related to the economic and legal privileges of the 'first class' – a class to which women were denied admittance. The consonance of aesthetic criteria with economic ones becomes clear in the term itself. The 'classics' of Athenian, Roman and Elizabethan drama were all produced by cultures that denied women access to the stage and allowed them few legal and economic rights. The values of a patriarchal society are embedded in the texts of these periods. Female characters reflect the absence of real women from the stage and the reasons for their absence. Each culture that regards it as valuable to revive those classic plays actively participates in the same patriarchal subtext which created those female characters as 'Woman'. Though we cannot examine an early production of a Greek classic, we can examine one of the 'classic' texts produced for the Dionysian festivals and still staged and studied in our own culture. *The Oresteia* exhibits all of the themes and practices discussed above. Moreover, its elevated position in the canon illustrates its lasting value. A feminist reading of *The Oresteia* illustrates the defeat of the old matriarchal genealogy, the nature of 'Woman' as portrayed on the stage, the rise of Athena and the legacy of the suppression of real women.

'The Oresteia'

Many feminist critics and historians have analysed *The Oresteia* as a text central to the formalisation of misogyny. Simone de Beauvoir and Kate Millett characterise the trilogy as the mythical rendering of a patriarchal takeover. Nancy Hartsock argues that it associates the female gender with sexuality and nature, those forces that must be tamed in outside activities and within the inner person for the survival of the *polis*.[11] Hartsock locates *The Oresteia* within the context of dramatic festivals themselves associated with male-gender activities. The drama, like the four-horse chariot race, is a contest. It formalises *agones* (contests) and the notion of winners and losers. The festivals associate the heroic ideal of valour in battle with the peace-time ideal of rhetorical and dramatic competition.[12] The subject of the drama is the subject of war – the male warrior hero. When this *agon* is inscribed with the conflicts of gender, the dramatic dice are loaded for the same gender-specific hero to win. *The Oresteia* enacts the 'battle of the sexes', using Athenian cultural and political codes to prescribe that women must lose the battle.

Early in the first play of the triology, *Agamemnon*, the chorus of old men explicates the dramatic situation within the perspective of male–female problems. The old men describe a promiscuous woman (Helen) as the cause of the Trojan War, in which Agamemnon is presently engaged, and tell of the war fleet launched as a result of Agamemnon's sacrifice of his virgin daughter Iphigenia. The Trojan War and the relationship of Agamemnon and Clytemnestra are already fraught with conflicts embedded in gender roles. Then the chorus prepares the audience for the entrance of Clytemnestra by linking gender with certain attributes of character. They suggest that steady resolve and intensity of purpose are gender-specific when they refer to the male (inner) strength of Clytemnestra (line 10).[13] Within this context Clytemnestra enters, played by a man. After she (he) speaks, the chorus congratulates her for thinking like a man and dismisses her announcement of the end of the war as just 'like a woman to take rapture before fact' (line 483). These lines presume certain gender roles regarding the judgement of evidence and decision-making. They also play with a certain level of irony founded on theatrical convention, since a man in drag plays a woman who 'thinks like a man'. Clearly, the primary referent is the male. The notion of the female, like the notion of the Amazon, disrupts the male order. Clytemnestra is introduced as a figure of that disruption. The absence of the male king has provided her with 'unnatural' political power. In his absence, she has taken a male lover. By this act, she disrupts the gender code of female sexuality, for the tradition was that women were to remain faithful to their husbands even during ten-year wars. The chorus treats Clytemnestra's liaison as dangerous. Yet, when Agamemnon enters with his sexual war booty, Cassandra, the text does not imply any social disruption. In fact, the dramatic pathos of the drama favours Agamemnon despite his brutal treatment of women, as evidenced by his rape of Cassandra and his murder of Iphigenia.

Cassandra provides the Athenian image of the woman in the public arena (even though she is played by a man). She has certain privileges of belonging (she is a priestess of Apollo, which assures her of sexual liaisons with citizens of rank such as Agamemnon), but she does not have the privilege of effective public speech because of her prior refusal to be violated by Apollo. Cassandra's entrance, as an outsider, as Agamemnon's booty, mute to Clytemnestra and expelled from effective dialogue, even portrayed by a male actor, projects the strength of the misogyny embedded in the Athenian patriarchal order. What remains in the play is only Clytemnestra's murder of Agamemnon and her complete vilification. At the end, the chorus mourns Agamemnon as one who had to fight a war for a woman and then be killed by one (lines 1453–4).

In the third play, *The Eumenides*, the winner of the battle of the sexes – in Athens and among the gods – is decided. From a feminist perspective, it is ironic that this play dramatises the so-called beginnings of democracy. Moreover, within theatre history, *The Eumenides* is often marked as the play of the new order of civilisation which created our Western tradition of reason and fair play. This may be an accurate designation in so far as Western civilisation has followed the deciding gender judgements of Athenian culture in condemning women to a subservient role. The play rests upon a new genealogy of the gods. It opens with the old order, the vile goddesses, the Furies (they become 'Eumenides' – the 'benevolent ones' – with their change of role at the end of the play). They create an ugly, frightening characterisation of the earlier chthonic female religions. The masks created for them were famous for their disgusting appearance. An extant remark about them states that they 'horrified women into miscarriages'[14] – an interesting anecdote for its gender and sexual connotations. The Furies have arrived in Athens, while pursuing Orestes to revenge his murder of his mother. They define their role as the punishment of matricide (line 210). Orestes appeals to Apollo for help and Athena appears to solve the problem. She institutes a trial, exhibiting Athenian methods of justice, to try Orestes for his murder. The decision is to set Orestes free. This conclusion is damning evidence for the public rationalisation of mysogyny, for it rests upon establishing the parental line as male. The mother is not the parent but the nurse of the child. The parent is defined as 'he who mounts' (lines 658–61). Athena is the supreme proof of this fact because she had no mother and was begotten by the male god Zeus (lines 734–8).

The Furies are confined to a cave and their function is no longer to revenge matricide, but to preside over marriages. Thus, the trilogy which began with the end of the Trojan War and followed the fortunes of the house of Agamemnon ends with the institution of democracy and decisions about gender roles and the rules governing procreation. This ending can be seen as paradigmatic of future plot structures in the Western play-writing tradition. A great many plays in the tradition resolve various kinds of civic, historical and psychological problems with the institution of marriage. The proper gender role for women is inscribed in this conclusion.

The feminist reader of *The Oresteia* discovers that she must read against the text, resisting not only its internal sense of pathos and conclusion, but also the historical and cultural codes which surround it, including its treatment within theatre history. The pathos the feminist reader feels may be for Iphigenia and Clytemnestra rather than for Agamemnon. She may perceive Athena as a male-identified woman in alliance with the male network of power rather than as a hero of Athens. She definitely feels excluded from the conventions of the stage, bewildered by the convention of cross-gender casting, which is only practised for female characters. Mimesis is not possible for her. Perhaps the feminist reader will decide that the female roles have nothing to do with women, that these roles should be played by men, as fantasies of 'Woman' as 'other' than man, as disruptions of a patriarchal society and illustrative of its fear and loathing of the female parts. In fact, the feminist reader might become persuaded that the Athenian roles of Medea, Clytemnestra, Cassandra and Phaedra are properly played as drag roles. The feminist reader might conclude that women need not relate to these roles or even attempt to identify with them. Moreover, the feminist historian might conclude that these roles contain no information about the experience of real women in the classical world. Nevertheless, the feminist scholar must recognise that theatre originated in this kind of cultural climate and that the Athenian experience will continue to provide a certain paradigm of theatrical practice for the rest of Western theatrical and cultural history. By linking practice, text and cultural background in this new way, she may enhance her understanding of how the hegemonic structure of patriarchal practice was instituted in Athens.

Aristotle

The legacy of the Greeks to theatre history does not end with the theatrical practice and texts of Athens. The process known as theatre was first and lastingly articulated by Aristotle in his *Poetics*. This text is still taught in theatre classes as the definitive source on the nature of classical tragedy. Based on the Greek practice as we have considered it and on the kind of texts produced for it, *The Poetics* expands the patriarchal prejudice against women to the nature of the dramatic experience and to the role of the audience.

Aristotle's perspective on women can be deduced from several of his criteria regarding the nature of dramatic character in chapter 15. The Golden translation reads, 'First and foremost, character should be good . . . goodness is possible for each class of individuals. For, both a woman and a slave have their particular virtues even though the former of these is inferior to a man, and the latter is completely ignoble' (lines 2–8).[15] Or, as the passage reads in the Else translation: 'In connection with the characters . . . first and most important, that they be good . . . but goodness exists in each class of people: there is in fact such a thing as a good woman and such a thing as a good slave, although no doubt one of these classes is inferior and the other, as a class, is worthless' (lines 54a16–24).[16] Aristotle begins his prescription for the tragic character with a moral imperative. In order to be tragic, one must be good. The absence of the male in his discussion illustrates that the male citizen is the standard of good, but that this quality may even be found in others. Aristotle relates goodness to class, but, more importantly, he relates class to gender. Slaves, as a class, are comparable to women, a gender. The class hierarchy, as he suggests it, assigns the highest status to male citizens, with female citizens somewhat inferior and slaves lowest of all. Although slaves are capable of goodness, they cannot be the subjects of tragedy, because they are 'ignoble' or 'worthless'. From the extant texts we know that Greek tragedy is the province of the royal houses. Women seem to occupy an ambiguous station. Though they may be subjects of tragedy, Aristotle implies that as subjects they are inferior to males.

Goodness is only the first quality of a dramatic character within *The Poetics*. Appropriate action is the second: the tragic character must perform actions appropriate to his character. As Else notes in his commentary, 'Appropriateness is not really a separate principle but a corollary to Aristotle's hierarchical view of goodness' (line 458). Thus, appropriateness of action is a quality of the noble character, as is goodness. Aristotle makes this point in reference to bravery and intellectual ability – characteristics appropriate to the tragic character. The Else translation reads, 'for it is possible for the character to be brave (manly) but not fitting to a woman (not by virtue of being brave or clever)' (lines 54a24–6). In the Golden translation: 'for it is possible for a person to be manly in terms of character, but it is not appropriate for a woman to exhibit either this quality or the intellectual cleverness that is associated with men' (lines 54a9–12). Else translates 'brave' and 'manly' as interchangeable terms, indicating that the male gender and bravery are one and the same. The same translation also indicates that a character is determined by gender, and that the tragic character is suited to the male gender, which connotes bravery. It is not appropriate for a woman to be manly – that is, to be brave and clever. The Golden translation does not explicitly mention bravery, but does mention 'intellectual cleverness'. Clearly, cleverness is a gender-specific quality necessary for the tragic character, but unavailable to women. Manliness, which connotes bravery to some, is another appropriate quality not to be found among women. Aristotle's assumptions rest upon the intersection of social reality and aesthetic prescriptions. In both realms, women are the outsiders. They function only to provide the limits of the male subject, which help to complete his outline, or they illustrate differences from him, which highlight his qualities. Once more, women are invisible – there are no qualities ascribed to them, and their invisibility provides the empty space which organises the focus on the male subject. In this way, they are subjects of tragic action only in so far as they might help to define the male character.

Beyond the requirements of character, however, women's supposed lack of intellectual cleverness may also exclude them from the entire experience of the drama, art or mimesis. In chapter 4, Aristotle links the act of representation to the pleasure of learning, both for the artist and for those who view his art: 'he learns his first lessons through imitation' and 'people enjoy seeing the reproductions: because in their viewing they find they are learning, inferring what class each object belongs to' (lines 48b15–17). The pleasure of mimesis is didactic, and learning is linked to the enjoyment–reception of its product. Since cleverness is gender-specific to the male, the enjoyment of art may be restricted to his province. Historians are uncertain about the composition of the Greek theatre audience. Some reason that, since it was restricted to full citizens, it is quite possible that no women were included. Others reason that, since Euripides jests about women in the audience in some of his plays, these jests constitute evidence of women's presence. Yet others reason that Euripides's tone of irony in all that he wrote makes it impossible to admit any of his statements as evidence. Judging from the gender-specific quality of Athenian theatre and Aristotle's thoughts on tragedy, it would seem likely that women were not in the audience; or, in the context of chapter 4, that they were present but ranked as inferior. In other words, not only was the male the practitioner of theatre and the ideal tragic character: he may also have been the exclusive recipient of the theatrical experience.

Moreover, the function of thought, in Aristotle's system, is to facilitate correct choices (lines 50b5–13). The function of pity, fear and recognition is to teach audiences about correct choices and to stimulate pleasure at the recognition. Not only are women counted as lacking the cleverness required to perceive these choices, but their powers of deliberation are discounted too. This idea is clearly articulated in Aristotle's *Politics*: 'the slave has no deliberative faculty at all; the woman has, but it is without authority'.[17] It is possible to conclude, then, that women have no need to learn about choices, since they are without the authority of choice; therefore, the drama has no function for them and they are excluded from the pleasure of watching it. Moreover, even dialogue would seem to be outside their realm – for, without authority, speaking is inappropriate, as the same passage in *The Politics* goes on to argue: 'the courage of a man is shown in commanding, but of a woman in obeying . . . as the poet says "Silence is a woman's glory", but this is not equally the glory of a man'.[18] Denied tragic qualities, cleverness, authority of deliberation and the right to speak, women seem to be excluded from the dramatic experience. The drama is not appropriate to the class of the gender of 'Woman'.

The feminist reader, identifying with her gender, finds herself reading against this text. In fact, she discovers that she is not even intended to be a reader of it. Whatever anger she may feel in reading Aristotle's insults, or whatever pity she may feel in identifying with the excluded women of the time, seems inappropriate given the exclusivity of this textual world. At this point, the feminist finds herself defined as one without the necessary qualifications for the study or the practice of the drama. The prominence of *The Poetics* within the history of the drama and the study of that history makes the exclusion of the feminist reader even more comprehensive. The feminist reader can, however, discover the methodology and assumptions of patriarchal production. She can begin to comprehend the alliance of theatre with patriarchal prejudice. The study of its development may inform the feminist analysis of contempoary theatre, assisting in the development of strategies to expose the fiction of 'Woman' in classic texts. The feminist theatre-practitioner might, for instance, understand *Lysistrata* not as a good play for women, but as a male drag show, with burlesque jokes about breasts and phalluses playing well in the drag tradition. The feminist director might cast a man in the role of Medea, underscoring the patriarchal prejudices of ownership and jealousy and the ownership of children as male concerns. The feminist actor may no longer regard these roles as desirable for her career. Overall, feminist practitioners and scholars may decide that such plays do not belong in the canon – and that they are not central to the study and practice of theatre.

The Elizabethan theatre

The Greek experience was replicated in the Elizabethan period in England, with the revalorisation of Aristotle's *Poetics*, conscious imitations of the classical writing-style and the assimilation of female roles by male actors. In England as in Athens, the earliest theatrical endeavours permitted some participation by women: during the Middle Ages, common women played in some local guild plays and wealthy women participated in some masques and tournaments. Yet, by the time theatre became a profession, women were once more banished from the stage. Again, this suppression of the public appearance of the female body and voice is rarely mentioned in studies of the period by historians and critics. The evidence for the evolution of the practice is minimal. In a central scholarly text on this period, *Early English Stages*, only a passing remark offers any reason for the exclusion of women from the stage. It suggests that, in the absence of civil or ecclesiastical decrees against women actors, their exclusion is probably to be explained by the weakness of women's voices, which were less suited to outdoor or cathedral acoustics, and by their lack of training in oratory.[19] Other critics suggest that women were excluded because they did not know how to read. The former theory simply enforces the notion that something in the biological make-up of women made them unsuited to public performance. Both theories fail to account for the exclusion of women from the kinds of training necessary for the stage.

The reason for the replication of the all-male theatre lies in the re-emergence of the Athenian compound of politics, myth and culture as assimilated by the Christian tradition. The predominantly Christian culture had revised the classical fiction of the female gender by locating it within the context of sexuality. The construction of the sexual frame for women in theatre had begun centuries earlier, when the Catholic Church banned the practice of theatre as immoral. Women who performed were associated with prostitution (a legacy from Greece and Rome). By the late Middle Ages, the Church had secured the notion that such immoral sexual conduct was the province of women: that is, that prostitutes caused prostitution. Therefore the control of prostitutes would control prostitution, or, more specifically, banning women from the stage would prevent the stage from becoming the site for immoral sexual conduct. The female gender had become the custodian of male sexual behaviour, which it instigated and elicited.[20] The female body had become the site for sexuality. If women performed in the public arena, the sexuality inscribed upon their bodies would elicit immoral sexual responses from the men, bringing disorder to the social body.

The classical creation of gender as opposites added another dimension to the oppression of the female gender in this period. Within Christian thought, the association of the female gender with sexuality was opposed by the association of the male gender with spirituality, leading to the practice of male celibacy as the context for cultural production. Thus, along with the suppression of the public appearance of the female gender, its metaphorical appearance in cultural productions became suppressed as well: the absence of women's voices in literature, philosophy, theology and other branches of learning was the counterpart of their absence from choirs and the stage. The oppositional model of gender resulted in the banning of women from the public offices of the Church, and from the schools, which during this period were all run by the Church. The equation of the female with sexuality as part of the model of gender opposites produced the condition described in *Early English Stages*: women were denied access to vocal training, the study of rhetoric and the written language. Along with the exclusion of the female gender as a cultural site and as a cultural producer, came the exclusion of the corporeal representation of sexuality, which had become associated with that gender. Without the public appearance of the female body, cultural representations of sexuality could not be physical ones. Rather, sexuality became located within the symbolic system that was the property of the spiritual domain – for instance, in language. Elizabethan theatre originated in these cultural codes and practices. Church schools and choirs supplied the first performers in this period, situating theatre within an all-male world which excluded the female–sexuality gender and practised celibacy. The stage could not be the site for corporeal representations of sexuality or desire, but must rely on language for its appearance. By the time of Shakespeare's plays, the theatre had ceased to be associated with Church-supported institutions and had moved into a secular realm of performance, but the nature of its roots was still evident.

In theatre, the sexual danger inherent in the female gender was alleviated by the male assimilation of female roles. In Shakespeare's theatre, the representation of the fiction of the female gender (and its concomitant sexuality) was assigned to boys. In fact, this period seemed to assign most theatrical performance to boys: it began with plays by choirboys and schoolboys, evolved into companies such as Shakespeare's, which employed both boys and men, and ended with the re-emergence of all-boy companies. Embedded in this intense theatrical focus on boys were certain solutions to the problem of the female–sexuality equation. In Shakespeare's theatre, certain qualities which Aristotle had earlier ascribed to women were attributed to boys. Compare this passage from Aristotle's *History of Animals* –

'the female is . . . more mischievous, less simple, more impulsive
. . . easily moved to tears . . . more deceptive'[21] – to a speech in
As You Like It. Rosalind tells Orlando how, as a boy, she had
taught a man to court a woman:

> He was to imagine me his love, his mistress: and I set him
> every day to woo me. At which time would I, being but a
> moonish youth, grieve, be effeminate, changeable, longing and
> liking, proud, fantastical, apish, shallow, inconstant, full of
> tears, full of smiles; for every passion something and for no
> passion truly anything, as boys and women are for the most
> part cattle of this colour.   (III.ii 378–89)

Boys, by virtue of their age, were cast in a social role similar to
that of women – dependent on and inferior to the adult male.
Women could be represented by boys on stage because they
shared their social attributes.

Shakespeare played upon this Elizabethan cultural practice by
foregrounding the practice of cross-gender casting in dramatic
scenes of love and desire – situations his period defined as crucial
to gender. Shakespeare further underscored this relationship
between cross-gender casting and sexuality by his use of triple-
gender-crossing in several of his comedies. In five plays (*Two
Gentlemen of Verona*, *The Merchant of Venice*, *As You Like It*,
Twelfth Night and *Cymbeline*), leading 'female' characters pretend
to be male. However, Shakespeare's plays on the boy–woman
exchange also participate in another sexual dynamic – the
representation of male homoeroticism. These comedies of love
focused on transvestite boys in erotic situations with other boys
or men. The celibacy of the stage was maintained by omitting the
presence of the female body and by representing physical sexuality
in the language. However, the boy–woman exchange produced
the erotic celebration of the boy in drag, whose language
eroticised his appearance. The above quotation from *As You
Like It* can be read for the alliance between cross-gender casting
and homoerotic flirtation. On one level, this flirtation scene is
actually played between two males: the boy actor who is playing
Rosalind and the boy or man playing Orlando. On another level,
a fictional woman, Rosalind, is flirting with Orlando while talking
to him as if she were a boy. On a third level, the dialogue

describes a courtship game played between a boy and a male lover who imagines that the boy is a woman. The wit and titillation of the passage enhance the ability of the transvestite boy successfully to negotiate a sexual liaison with another male. The fictional 'Woman' (the character of Rosalind) simply mediates and enhances the homoerotic flirtation between two males.

Shakespeare further extends this transvestite flirtation to the audience. The same boy actor as plays Rosalind returns to deliver the epilogue, revealing himself as a boy and flirting directly with the men in the audience:

> I'll begin with the women, for the love you bear to men, to like as much of this play as please you: and I charge you, O men, for the love you bear to women . . . that between you and the women the play may please. If I were a woman I would kiss as many of you as had beards that pleased me, complexions that liked me and breaths that I defied not: and, I am sure, as many as have good beards or good faces or sweet breaths will, for my kind offer, when I make curtsy, bid me farewell.

After a summary tribute to heterosexuality, the boy actor reveals himself as a boy, yet continues to invoke his fictional gender as a woman to suggest that he would kiss the men. Note that he does not make any such flirtatious remark to the women in the audience – in fact, they are used only to foreground the men as the objects of desire. After his coy list of good beards, faces and sweet breaths, as the boy actor, he curtsies (an action assigned to the female gender) and exits. This epilogue illustrates a point Lisa Jardine makes in *Still Harping on Daughters*: 'Whenever Shakespeare's female characters in the comedies draw attention to their own androgyny . . . the resulting eroticism is to be associated with their maleness rather than their femaleness.'[22]

Further evidence of Shakespeare's stage as the site for homoeroticism appears in the Puritan anxiety about it. In fact, the Puritan reaction against the decadence of the stage was often related directly to this practice. While Puritan documents cannot be considered as unbiased accounts, they do provide information about both homoerotic and misogynistic anxieties of the period. Several extant Puritan sermons were built upon a quotation in Deuteronomy (22:5) which specifically forbade cross-dressing:

'The woman shall not wear that which pertaineth unto a man, neither shall a man put on a woman's garment; for all that do so are an abomination unto the Lord thy God.' The Puritans concentrated on clear gender distinctions and their relation to heterosexuality. The Puritans recorded their perceptions that boys in the female parts encouraged homoerotic responses by members of the audience who 'have been desperately enamored with Players Boys thus clad in woman's apparell, so far as to solicit them by words, by letters, etc.' (from *Histrio-mastix: The Players Scourge or Actors Tragedie*, 1632). Some Puritans, such as Philip Stubbes, suggested that the boys were 'Sodomites', citing their 'lewd adulterous kisses and embracements' upon the stage (*Anatomy of Abuses*, 1583). Though these reactions may have misplaced the titillation from language to physical behaviour, overlooking the function of artifice, they do record a perception that the homoerotic dynamic was employed for the entertainment of the audience.

Some traditional critics articulate this same perception in a more polite, literary context, using the framework of aesthetics to legitimate it. Harley Granville-Barker argues that Shakespeare's theatre produced a 'celibate stage'. Focusing on the absence of physical representations of sexuality, he describes *Antony and Cleopatra* as 'a tragedy of sex without one single scene of sexual appeal', further asserting that Shakespeare discovered that 'the true stuff of tragedy and of the liveliest comedy lies beyond sensual bounds'.[23] This kind of interpretation legitimises the exclusion of women from the stage and the homoerotic nature of the transvestite boy by emphasising the formality or stylisation of acting demanded by the all-male stage. The argument insists that this transvestism intensified the artifice of the stage, foregrounding its aesthetic frame. Its proponents often cite a passage from Goethe, on seeing men playing women's roles: 'the idea of imitation, the thought of art was called forth vividly . . . a kind of self-conscious illusion was produced'.[24] This patriarchal critical tradition of aestheticising male transvestitism on the stage rests upon the same principles the Church used to exclude women in the first place: that the male gender within the practice of celibacy is the appropriate site for public performance and artistic production. Aesthetics merely replaces spirituality in this formula, insisting that the male appropriation of the female role, which stifles the physical playing of sexuality, transferring it to the symbolic system of language, is the source of the aesthetics of theatre. In other words, the argument asserts that the boy Juliet is somehow more aesthetic, more central to the practice of theatre, than a female one. Tragedy and comedy lie 'beyond sensual bounds', which means beyond the bounds of the female actor, who is sensual by nature of her gender. This is what Jan Kott more appropriately termed 'Shakespeare's bitter Arcadia', where the boy androgyne has the freedom to play the puns and tropes of homoerotic flirtation.[25]

Ironically, the feminist studies of Shakespeare which have proliferated in the last decade largely ignore this practice and its insidious implications for women. With the exception of Lisa Jardine, the scholars in question keep primarily to the earlier feminist critical practice of reading the images of women within the text, ignoring the exclusion of women actors to represent them. This approach is evident in titles such as *Shakespeare's Women*, *Comic Women*, *Tragic Men* and *The Woman's Part*. Reading within the text rather than within the practice, most of these works, concentrating on the images of independent women in the comedies and contrasting them with the negative images of women in the tragedies, characterise Shakespeare's portrayals of women as ahead of his time, or the best of his time. Though several of these works include small sections on the boy actor, few really read the implications of cross-gender casting into the text – in fact, some see the practice in a positive light: 'it results from Shakespeare's ability to see through the limitations of conventional gender expectations'; or, 'for the boy actor of female characters: playing women can itself be maturing'.[26] These feminist critics do not deconstruct the powerful misogyny found in the image of a man playing Lady Macbeth and saying 'unsex me', nor do they account for the double negative in *Twelfth Night*, in which two boys court one another, playing female characters.

Unlike the Greek audience, Shakespeare's certainly included women as well as men. Critics such as Granville-Barker would have their readers believe that women in the audience better appreciated the artifice of theatre through seeing Juliet and her nurse portrayed by a boy and an older man. It causes the modern theatre scholar to wonder how the age understood female beauty

when Cleopatra was played by a boy. Did the women perceive
the stage in the way the Puritans did – as a homoerotic game?
Did they become voyeurs watching the flirtations of Shakespeare's
boys? What sense did women have of their own sexuality?
Perhaps they concluded that the message these plays offered was
that women are only sexual as boys. The doubling of cross-gender
dressing in *As You Like It* and *Twelfth Night* may have encouraged
them to think that women could only woo, play and engage in
sexual games as boys. After all, the endings of the comedies may
be interpreted not as illustrating the way in which heterosexual
marriage confirms the order of society, but as confirming that,
within Shakespeare's stage practice, males marry each other, so
producing a sense of narrative and dramatic closure.

What, then, does the fictional female in Shakespeare imply?
Fictional 'Woman' here emerges clearly as an object of exchange
between men: 'Women, signs, goods, currency, all pass from one
man to another.'[27] The character of Rosalind in *As You Like It* is
an object of exchange within a homoerotic economy. She is
created to allow the boy actor playing her to play a boy in his
flirtation scenes with Orlando. The fiction is necessary to negotiate
the taboo against homosexuality, exchanging it for the value of
artifice – the aesthetic of the stage. This makes the fictional
female upon the stage the merchandise necessary to facilitate
erotic exchange, the sex object which mediates trade between
two sexual subjects. Perhaps an exploration of this level of
exchange could amplify the levels of meaning in *The Merchant of
Venice*, where money, exchange and marriage are clearly linked.
For example, Portia's father has placed her image within one of
three caskets – gold, silver and lead. Her suitors must choose the
correct casket in order to attain her and her money (through her
image) or remain forever celibate. The image of the woman is
placed within what is in effect a vessel for currency: the male may
attain sexuality through the exchange of the female image or
must live the celibate life – a situation reflecting the conditions of
the Elizabethan stage.

Shakespeare's stage acted out the central anxieties and codes of
the period concerning sexuality and the female gender. For a
while, the stage offered a cultural construction which seemed to
ensconce these elements in the safety of artifice. The boy actor
could enact the sex object, powerful in cross-dress, but basically

dependent. The celibacy of this stage and the dependence of the boy maintained the female sex object as one without any real power or danger. Real women were invisible in the offices of the Church, the majority of schools and standard theatrical performances. This solution began to weaken when the Catholic Church no longer dominated spirituality. The rise of the Puritans broke the solution of celibacy. The close of the theatres removed the safety of artifice. Boys no longer represented women – the fiction of the female gender was applied to real women. The cultural fictions which had served to suppress women gave way to the witch hunts, in which real women were murdered and tortured for the supposed sins of their gender. When the theatres reopened, women were allowed to play the female roles. In fact, when female actors appeared on the stage, bawdy comedies and narratives of lust began to dominate the theatres. The fiction of the female gender had been securely inscribed on real women. This age marked a transition from the virgin goddess Athena (and the virgin queen Elizabeth) to the sex goddess of the twentieth century. Either way, women did not escape the role of merchandise in the world of male exchange.

Chapter 2

Women Pioneers

For most of the history of patriarchal culture, ownership of property, the public arena, written language and theatre itself have been exclusively, or almost exclusively, male. For centuries the theatrical achievements of women remained largely invisible. The few women whose achievements made them visible emerged from a host of invisible and forgotten women, who, one can only assume, included creative and productive artists and performers. The few women who have entered the annals of early theatre history were usually privileged in some way: by class, by their beauty, by their association with men of influence, or perhaps because their work manifested some similarities with the works in the canon. In other words, even among women, class, race, sexual and social contacts and conformity to patriarchal codes have created great differences. The performances and narratives of poor women, women of colour, lesbians, 'unattractive' women and innovative women, who may have experimented in forms suited to their own private world rather than those of the public patriarchal one, were not considered significant in the history of theatre by virtue of the dominant cultural codes. Yet even the work of the so-called 'elite' women is only scantily documented. For this reason, the present chapter will offer a sampling of women playwrights who played a pioneering role in the history of women in the theatre. However, since women were largely excluded from the dominant culture, the history of their part in theatre history must differ substantially from that of men. Any history of women in performance must include achievements in performance areas which originated in the unique experiences of women. Alongside traditional categories of production such as playwriting, directing and designing, consideration must be given to modes of performance located in the domestic and personal spheres which were assigned to women by the patriarchy.

With this in mind, the history of women playwrights should take into account evidence from outside the history of written texts. A re-examination of the term 'playwright' explicates the point. The etymology of the word, its literal definition, provides a wider arena in which to work than just the discovery of written texts. 'Wright' does not denote writing, but means someone who makes something, an artificer. In other words, a playwright is a *maker* of plays, not necessarily a *writer* of plays. This understanding extends the search for women playwrights to the first women in history who 'made' plays. The first women playwrights created in the medium their cultures allowed them – the language of the body. These were the women mimes who performed in the market places, the streets and before the theatres in classical Greece and Rome. Their theatre tradition was a silent one, consisting of physical dramatic invention. Their bodies were the sites of their texts. They were denied the permanency of the written text, along with its privileged association with theatre buildings, state revenues and pools of professional performers, all of which were available to men. Yet their performances were central enough in the culture for them to be included in the texts of theatre history. Unfortunately, there was no technique for recording these wordless events – not until highly sophisticated playwrights such as Samuel Beckett was there the concept of a written script without formal speech. However, we know from the study of the *commedia dell'arte* and the theatre of Molière that there has been a tradition of wordless 'scripts' based on stock characters and situations. These later examples illustrate how, without writing, material was saved, sculpted, revised and repeated until it 'worked' before an audience. Therefore, the successful mimes, who performed regularly in front of the public in Greece and Rome were making plays.

What kinds of plays were these women making and what is their contribution to theatre history? Scholars suggest that the mimes included satires on local personalities and current events as well as popular versions of the myths. Since the written theatre of Greece was restricted to Greek citizens, the Greek mimes were the founders of popular theatre, performing for the people who were denied access to the state theatre and to written texts. Moreover, these mimes were the founders of street theatre, performing where people congregated. They were the first performers to explore alternative performance spaces – adapting their material to the space. They may also have influenced written texts, in ways that were never recorded. Perhaps these silent women playwrights created dramatic devices and specific dramatic moments that were assimilated by the male playwrights of their time. For example, classical comedy may have borrowed its comic types or its themes for topical satire from those which emerged on the street. Perhaps even specific scenarios were borrowed from them. Perhaps a playwright such as Aristophanes was adept at setting the inventions of these mimes and dancers to words, in the same way as Charlie Chaplin influenced Brecht, or Buster Keaton inspired Beckett. Since classical Greek and Roman theatre did not privilege original narratives, the playwrights of the written word may have borrowed from the silent traditions of their times as well as from the oral traditions of the myths.

Within a feminist context, these women mimes may be identified as playwrights. However, the patriarchal theatre histories generally refer to them as 'actress–courtesans', appending the sexual role ascribed to the female gender to the description of women performers. A feminist approach can suggest several ways to interpret the implications of this word 'courtesan'. It may describe the male desire aroused by the sight of the female body in performance, especially since it was limited to these mimes. In other words, the male desire projected upon the female performer created the image of the woman as 'courtesan'. Interestingly, in Greece public performance by women connoted illicit sexual activity, while public performance by men – even athletes, who regularly competed in the nude – did not. However, these mimes were slaves – outside the privileges of economic exchange and property. Perhaps they did have to sell their bodies as well as their performances. The role of 'courtesan' may have been the only source of independent wealth for women in the classical period. We know that some of the Roman women mimes became wealthy in this way. It seems that their access to this wealth threatened the Roman social system so much that laws were created to prevent them from passing on their wealth to their children.

Yet it is difficult to evaluate the connection, during this period, between selling the body and performing in public. Without knowing the sexual habits of male performers and playwrights, it is difficult to determine whether or not all theatre people combined performance with sexual favours, or whether the practice was limited to women. Given the history of male homosexuality in Greece, it is quite possible that the granting of sexual favours was linked to participation in the dramatic festivals, or that on such grounds the *archontes* (chief magistrates) personally favoured some playwrights and saw to it that their works were performed. From another perspective, the selling of sexual favours might have been a typical practice of both genders of the slave class. Again, without the evidence of male sexual practices, it is unclear whether the role of 'courtesan' was limited to women slaves who performed. Nevertheless, there is evidence that some of the Roman women mime artists were courtesans.

The image of the actress–courtesan reached its symbolic and legal peak in the life of Theodora, during the fifth century AD. Though biographical details about her are limited primarily to her sexual and romantic liaisons, they still convey some sense of the life of an early woman playwright.

Theodora was a famous mime and dancer who began entertaining in her childhood. She began performing in the Imperial Circus at Constantinople, where her father was a bear-keeper. She rose to prominence as a dancer known for her erotic sensibility. At the height of her career as an entertainer, the Emperor Justinian fell in love with her and wished to marry her. However, the law decreed that actress courtesans could not become Roman citizens and thus could not become the legal wives of citizens. Justinian's desire, along with the new Christian concepts of repentance and salvation, produced the edict of 521 AD which declared that actress–courtesans could repent, renounce their profession and become the legal wives of Roman citizens. The marriage of Theodora symbolises a crucial transition in women's theatre history: the passing of the classical tradition of the actress–courtesan and the rise of Christianity, which assured women spiritual mobility (they could be saved) and forbade theatrical performance. The symbolic significance of Theodora informed the works of the first woman known to have written plays – Hrotsvit von Gandersheim.

Hrotsvit von Gandersheim

Hrotsvit von Gandersheim is the first known woman playwright of written texts – an identity which has taken one thousand years to emerge and which has yet to be placed within a critical and historical perspective. She adopted the name Hrotsvit, which means 'strong voice'. She spent her life working in a convent in Gandersheim – thus the name Hrotsvit von Gandersheim. This 'strong voice' wrote her plays in the Holy Roman Empire, in what is now known as Germany. She wrote other works as well. In fact, Hrotsvit was the poet laureate of the Empire. She wrote in the mid-tenth century at a time when there was no theatre in Western Europe. She wrote six plays as a feminist revision of the misogynistic images of women in the plays of the Roman playwright Terence. She clearly states her project in the preface to her plays: 'Wherefore I, the strong voice of Gandersheim, have not hesitated to imitate a poet [Terence] whose works are so widely read, my object being to glorify, within the limits of my poor talent, the laudable chastity of Christian virgins in that self-same form of composition which has been used to describe the shameless acts of licentious women.'[1] In other words, she undertook to change the negative roles assigned to women in the classical plays to the positive roles of Christian women.

Women are at the centre of the plays' action and it is their alternative to patriarchal sexual possession which determines the development of the plots. Hrotsvit places her heroines in the classical context of objectification, use and violence, but offers them an alternative context for their choices. Chastity is portrayed as a declaration of independence from prescribed marriages, attempted rape and all acts of male sexual aggression which ignore women's consent. For example, the play *Dulcitius* opens with three young women before the Emperor Diocletian and his soldiers. Diocletian declares the patriarchal edict: 'The pure and famous race to which you belong and your own rare beauty make it fitting that you should be wedded to the highest in the court.' Yet, despite the rank and military power behind this edict, the young girls resist, replying that they have vowed to live a chaste life. Angered, the Emperor sends them to prison in the charge of Governor Dulcitius. Dulcitius wants to seduce them because of their beauty, but the guards warn him that the women will resist seduction. He responds, 'Then I shall woo in another fashion – with torture!' First, however, Dulcitius attempts to rape them. As he enters the prison, a spell overcomes him and he makes love to the pots and pans, thinking that they are the women. This scene provides a witty comment on the confusion of male desire. Dulcitius cannot distinguish women from the tools of their domestic trade. His would-be victims observe his silly thrashing about, giggling and whispering among themselves. It seems that the women will overcome the rapist. Yet ensuing scenes portray the torture and murder of the women by the army. Nevertheless, the women are still the victors within Hrotsvit's Christian world, for they all overcome their death as they ascend to heaven. The play ends during the ascension of one of them, who shames the soldiers for performing such brutal, ultimately ineffectual acts against vulnerable young girls. Ultimately, the young women are the victors, for they never marry, in spite of humiliation, torture and death. The victory of these women over the savage oppression of the patriarchy marks the strength of their wills and the freedom of consent in the choice of chastity.

The play *Callimachus* also centres on rape and consent. In the opening scenes, Callimachus tells Drusiana he loves her because of her beauty. She responds with incomprehension: 'My beauty? What is my beauty to you?' This is a provocative question within the patriarchal economy of desire. Nevertheless, Callimachus concludes that he will use all of his skill and strength to trap her. Drusiana begs Christ to help her to die so that she may escape her dilemma. Christ complies with her wishes immediately – women have the power to petition and succeed. The following scene is chilling in its dramatisation of the extremes of the sexual objectification of women. Callimachus enters Drusiana's tomb in order to rape her corpse. Hrotsvit has cast the passive sexual role assigned to women in the context of full-blown perversion. But Callimachus is killed by a heaven-sent serpent before he can complete the act. Later Drusiana is resurrected and she in turn resurrects Callimachus, converting him to her world view. The plot is moved in her direction and by her resolve.

Hrotsvit's most famous play is based on a woman like Theodora.

In fact, it was probably inspired by the image of Theodora. The play is entitled *Paphnutius*, but it centres on the dancer–courtesan Thais. This play is an intricate interweaving of medieval scholastic philosophy and dramatic devices, displaying the sophistication of Hrotsvit's education and philosophical training. Thais's illicit sexuality and erotic dancing disrupt the internal peace of the monastic community. This peace cannot be restored until Thais gives up the assimilation of her sexuality to financial gain (prostitution), which alienates her body from her soul. This is the first play by a woman playwright that dramatises the feminist notion that women must reclaim their own bodies in order to establish their internal health. The play begins with an exposition of the contiguity among all the parts of the world, through the organisation of musical harmony, in the combination of body and soul and 'even in the pulsation of the veins and in the proportion of our members'. Because of this contiguity, Paphnutius (a monk in a distant monastery) cannot find inner peace until Thais (a courtesan in a distant city) restores the concord between her sexuality and her inner feelings. In other words, the sexual objectification of women disrupts the entire community. The following scenes dramatise the new dynamic of repentance and salvation that were available to women. Thais acts out the inner life of meditation and mystic contemplation which brings her to her final ascension. Hrotsvit has created the first image of a woman's internal life to be written by a woman playwright and to survive in the annals of theatre history.

All Hrotsvit's plays are written in a unique style that resembles the intense reduction of dialogue found in such contemporary authors as Beckett or Kroetz. The plays are episodic, with some scenes consisting of as little as three lines of dialogue. Hrotsvit relies on the contiguity and interdependence of all things in the universe to draw the necessary relationships among scenes. This principle of contiguity rather than linear development has been hailed by some feminist critics as the basis of a distinctively feminine morphology. These ideas will be developed more fully in Chapter 7, but for the moment it may be said that Hrotsvit's style may be in line with such a distinctively female form of the drama – making her role as pioneer woman playwright central to the tradition of women playwrights.

Hrotsvit's plays may have been performed in her convent

during her lifetime. There is no evidence either to support or to deny this possibility. If they were performed, the performances marked an auspicious beginning for women's plays: written by a woman playwright and produced by women for an all-woman audience within the context of a female community. Subsequently, there have been few productions of her plays. They were not collected for circulation until the sixteenth century, were not translated from medieval Latin into modern Romance languages until the mid nineteenth century, and did not become available in English until the twentieth century. The relative unavailability of her texts made production improbable. Even today, Hrotsvit's plays are out of print. The only available translations into English are those published in 1923 by Christabel Marshall under the pseudonym 'Christopher St John'. Yet Hrotsvit did enjoy a certain popularity in London during the years of the suffragette movement. The first major production of *Paphnutius* was directed by Edith Craig (daughter of Ellen Terry and sister of Gordon) in London in 1914. The play was staged by Edith Craig's own ensemble, the Pioneer Players, with Ellen Terry as Thais. In 1920 there was a production of *Callimachus* at the Art Theatre, and in 1924 a production of *Paphnutius* at the Maddermarket Theatre, Norwich. In 1926 the Roswitha Club was formed and new translations by Waley and Tillyard were published. With the exception of one production in the 1920s by a women's theatre group in New York, productions of Hrotsvit in the United States have been limited to college theatres.

One need only contrast Hrotsvit's production record with that of Aeschylus (the first male playwright in the Western tradition) in order to perceive the prejudice of stage practice. Excluding Hrotsvit from theatrical production suppresses the importance of the first woman playwright. This suppression produces a reciprocal depression of values – both the pioneer of the tradition and those who follow receive only minor regard. On the one hand, contemporary women's plays are more likely to be excluded from the canon because they appear not to have any precedent and do not follow a discernible tradition of development, and, on the other, the position of the pioneer continues to be ignored because there is no discernible tradition of development which springs from her initial model. Production ensures the reception of plays by accustoming audiences to certain conventions. For example, audiences are accustomed to Aeschylus's mythological universe of Olympian gods and Greek heroes and find no need to take it literally. However, because of the lack of productions, audiences tend to treat Hrotsvit's Christian mythology not as a convention of the time but as a narrow and limiting description of the universe. Thus, Hrotsvit continues to be identified by critics and historians as the first author of 'school drama' (Brockett) or 'a minor eulogist of ordinary Christian heroes'.[2] It is left to feminist critics and historians to develop Hrotsvit's role as the founder of a tradition of women writing for the theatre.

Aphra Behn and Susanna Centlivre

Hrotsvit remained an anomaly for 700 years. The next women to write plays that would survive in the history of theatre wrote in the seventeenth century. However, in contrast to Hrotsvit's plays, the plays of these women have survived because of their outstanding success in production. Aphra Behn was the first woman to make her living as a playwright. She wrote eighteen plays and all of them were staged in major London theatres. Several of them enjoyed impressive runs: *The Busy Body* had over 450 performances before 1800 and became a stock piece in the nineteenth century; *The Wonder!* was performed over 250 times before 1800, with the role of Don Felix played by Garrick (one of the most distinguished actors of his time) more than sixty-five times between 1756 and 1776. Behn's most successful play, *The Rover*, held the stage from 1677 until 1760.

Aphra Behn described herself as 'an author who is forced to write for bread and not ashamed to own it'.[3] This condition distinguishes her from the many contemporaries of hers who wrote for the stage in gentlemanly leisure: of the fifteen living dramatists who had two or more plays produced at that time, two were earls, one was a duke, four were knights and one was a baron. Other playwrights, though not necessarily nobility, were educated at Oxford and enjoyed the benefits of 'good' families. Behn was a poor woman. She was widowed at a young age and forced to find some way to support herself. Her first employment was as a British spy. The government sent her to Holland to spy on troop movements during the Dutch wars. Once in Holland, she found that the government was not forthcoming with its funds – she could not even pay the travel expenses she had incurred – so she borrowed money to return to London. When she returned in 1667, she discovered that London had been ravaged by the Great Fire. People were without homes and food and her debtors were demanding immediate compensation. Without funds, she was sentenced to debtors' prison. There are no clear records of her release, but we know that her first play, *The Forced Marriage*, was produced in 1670 at Lincoln's Inn Fields. It is unclear how Behn conceived the idea of writing plays for money. Some critics suggest that it might have been because a woman, Katherine Philips, had just enjoyed a lucrative run of her translation of Corneille's *Pompey* (1663). Yet the success of a single translation seems less than inspiring. Perhaps Behn noted the success male playwrights were enjoying at the time. For a woman, writing must have seemed to provide an easier access to independence than mercantile ventures. Whatever the inspiration, Behn clearly wrote 'for bread' and succeeded quite handsomely at it for several years. Behn's contemporary critics sneered at her self-professed pecuniary goal, suggesting that she was a 'hack' writer, guided more by money than aesthetics. Yet her role as a professional writer has been an inspiration to several twentieth-century women authors who looked to history for role models. Virginia Woolf in *A Room of One's Own* wrote, 'here begins the freedom of the mind . . . for now that Aphra Behn had done it, girls could say "I can make money by my pen" '.[4]

Though Behn's plays enjoyed financial success, they did not earn critical success – either in her lifetime or after. Her plays have been regarded as imitative (*Sir Patient Fancy* as plagiarised from Molière's *Malade imaginaire*) and as simply stock characters in stock situations. Ironically, these weaknesses are often applauded as strengths of Molière himself, who borrowed both his plots and stock characters from the *commedia*. The harshest criticism offered against Behn's plays, both at the time and later, is that they are too bawdy. Behn responded to this criticism as gender bias: 'it is the least and most excusable fault in the men writers . . . but from a woman it was unnatural'.[5] Behn wrote plays the audiences wanted to see – her plays were the kind of plays which were successful in the theatres of her time. She set scenes in brothels (for instance, in *The Town Fop*) and created happy scenes between illicit lovers, even as they were just getting out of bed (*The Forced Marriage*). These scenes are situated in the domain of women. As sexualised objects of their society, their realms of power and development were the bedrooms and brothels. Women lived in the spheres of sexual and marital arrangements, deriving their personal power from liaisons with men. If these situations are bawdy, they are bawdy for men, who had the liberty of the public sphere. For women, they were simply the only realm of potential narrative and dialogue.

Behn regarded writing bawdy scenes as part of the freedom of the playwright, as well as part of the very tradition of comedy. In defence of *The Lucky Chance*, which was attacked for its immorality, she wrote, 'All I ask is the privilege for my masculine part the poet in me . . . to take those measures that both the ancient and modern writers have set me . . . if I must not, because of my sex, have this freedom, but that you will usurp all to yourselves; I lay down my quill and you shall hear no more of me.'[6] These lines exhibit the militancy and strength Behn asserted to make her way into the male province of theatre. Behn wrote many such attacks on male privilege and gender bias in her prologues, epilogues and letters. These statements are part of her legacy to the women playwrights and critics who follow her. She articulated the struggle which is necessary for a woman if she is to succeed at writing plays, getting them produced and surviving the gender-biased attacks of the critics. Behn created a model of resistance for the woman playwright.

In the past decade, there have been new critical works on Behn and new productions of her plays. Undoubtedly, this is an outgrowth of the new interest in women playwrights created by the feminist movement. Yet thorough rereadings of her plays and of her entire opus have yet to appear. A feminist critic could deconstruct the traditional evaluation of her work, re-viewing the treatment of women in her plays, the resonance of her themes and the aptness of her settings. New productions of her plays within a different context for production and reception, could highlight the uniqueness of Behn's legacy to the theatre, beyond her fight for equality and financial success.

Through her persistence and success, Behn opened the way for many women playwrights of her period to achieve financial success in the theatre. During the period from 1660 to 1720, over sixty plays by women were produced on the London stage – more than from 1920 to 1980.[7] Twenty of these plays were written by Susanna Centlivre.

More prolific than Behn, Centlivre introduced new images of women to the stage – a project Behn did not undertake. Perhaps Centlivre's life provided her with experiences which allowed for a more unique and daring sense of possibilities for female characters. She left home at age sixteen and lived part of her youth as a boy. In drag as 'Cousin Jack', she frequented the university, attending classes in fencing, grammar, logic, rhetoric, and so on. Living in a cross-gender role provided her with an education and a set of adventures useful to a promising playwright. Life in drag was not uncommon for women in seventeenth-century London. As early as 1610 the play *The Roaring Girl* by Middleton and Dekker documented the life of Moll Frith – a woman who lived in drag and made her living through her skill with the sword. At the time of Centlivre, Hortense Mancini was living in London in drag and demonstrating her fencing-skills in St James's Park. Aphra Behn had already written drag scenes for women in *The Amorous Prince* and *Sir Timothy Tawdry*. Most critics have regarded these roles as imitations of Shakespeare, but they may have been based upon the lives and practices of real women. Centlivre also wrote some scenes for women in drag. They differ a great deal from Shakespeare's. They are not happy, witty scenes set in forests such as Arden; rather, they are dark, desperate scenes in which women cross-dress to gain the power or freedom to express their wills. For example, in *The Perjur'd Husband* (1700), Centlivre's first play, Placentia dresses as a man to gain access to her husband's new mistress. When she determines that the woman is guilty of consciously stealing her husband, she reveals herself as a woman and stabs her to death. Unlike in Shakespeare, the use of drag in Centlivre does not resolve social issues (as it does for Portia in *The Merchant of Venice*), but demonstrates the anger and desperation of the female character. For women, the necessity of male disguise caused privation and anxiety. The Moll Friths and the young Centlivres experienced the fear of discovery and the social distaste for their roles. Yet, in order to gain access to education or daring physical action, they were required to don men's apparel. An examination of a modern play about women who live as men, *The Singular Life of Albert Nobbs*, appears in the final chapter of this book. This play, written during the years of the feminist movement, explores the internal experiences of women such as these.

Possibly the role reversal in Centlivre's real life provided her with the viewpoint of an independent woman who lived outside the social order. Centlivre creates independent female characters who invent unusual social roles for themselves. Sometimes, as when the heroine in *The Beau's Duel* adopts the role of the sexual pursuer, they assume social roles identified with men; but Centlivre's most unique character is Valeria, 'a philosophical girl', in *The Basset Table* (1705). Valeria is both the brunt of the play's humour and the victorious exception to the social code. She makes her first entrance in pursuit of a fly, worrying that she will 'lose the finest insect for dissection, a huge fresh fly, which Mr Lovely sent me just now, and opening the box to try the experiment, away it flew'.[8] The other characters on stage berate her for the unwomanly pursuit of such studies, but she defends herself well. Finally, one lady advises her to found 'a college for the study of philosophy, where none but women should be admitted; and to immortalize your name, they should be called "Valerians" '. Valeria responds, 'What you make a jest of, I'd execute, were it in my power.'[9] Centlivre's portrayal of a college for women has both a dramatic force and a comic eccentricity in its treatment – not unlike her own illicit attendance of classes at the university as a boy. Valeria, like herself, is the forceful outsider – a woman who wants to live by her intelligence. Centlivre provides a poignant and comic portrait of such a woman in 1705.

Both Centlivre and Behn provide social, domestic portraits of the women of their time. For financial and aesthetic reasons, they write in the traditional forms of the theatre of their time, exploiting the possibilities they afforded for female dialogue and narrative. Their biographies offer interesting portraits of women in their time. They were both poor women who made their way in a financial world reserved for men and upon a stage which had only recently allowed even the female actor. Three recent books provide useful material on these playwrights: Maureen Duffy's *The Passionate Shepherdess*, Fidelis Morgan's *The Female Wits* and Nancy Cotton's *Women Playwrights in England*. Behn and Centlivre were pioneers as women writing and producing plays.

Hopefully, the next decade of feminist history and criticism will provide useful work on their plays.

Sor Juana Inés de la Cruz

Sor Juana was the first woman playwright in the New World to write plays that were performed and published. Sor (sister) Juana was a nun in the Order of St Jerome in Mexico. Born in 1651, she was the illegitimate child of two members of the court. She spent her early years in the village of San Miguel de Nepantla, which is located just outside of Mexico City by the famous volcanoes Popocatepetl and Ixtaccihuatl. Sor Juana's single passion in life was to think and learn. She relates her intellectual autobiography in her most famous work, *La Respuesta* or *The Reply*. This work was the last document she would write, for it was a reply to the attack on her by the Bishop of Puebla criticising her for her focus on intellectual activity and her study of profane works. After her brilliant reply, Sor Juana dispersed her famous personal library and ceased her studies. *The Reply* stands as one of the most important historical documents in defence of women's intellectual abilities and love of learning. She describes her passion: 'from the moment I was first illuminated by the light of reason, my inclination toward letters has been so vehement, so overpowering, that not even the admonitions of others – and I have suffered many – nor my own meditations – and they have not been few – have been sufficient to cause me to forswear this natural impulse'.[10] Sor Juana learned to read and write at the age of six. Later, when she learned that there was a university in Mexico City, she pleaded with her mother to allow her to dress as a boy and attend classes. When her mother refused, she began to educate herself in her grandfather's library. By the time she was sixteen, she was honoured at court for her brilliance. A day was set aside during which members of the court could ask her questions, or listen to her read from her works.

Sor Juana was primarily a poet, but she enjoyed the production of her first play when she was eight years old. She wrote one full-length play in the secular tradition of the *commedia* entitled *Los Empeños de una casa* (the title is a play on a title by Calderón, difficult to translate into English). The play is a typical plot of intrigue and love, with sly servants and passionate lovers. She also wrote three *autos sacramentales*, which are allegorical plays about the mystery of the sacrament of the Eucharist, written to educate the masses and performed with lavish costumes and sets. Perhaps her most interesting plays are her short *loas*, plays which introduce the longer *autos*. These plays make Sor Juana the pioneer of ethnic theatre, since, unlike her male colonial counterparts, she incorporates the sights and sounds of indigenous ritual into some of her *loas*.

The *loa* to *The Divine Narcissus* (*El Divino Narciso*) introduces two Indians in full tribal costume – a man named Occident and a woman named America. The play begins with Indian dances and songs to the god of the seeds. The two characters praise the powers of their god and his ceremony of blood sacrifice, describing entrails and palpitating hearts which have been cut from the victims. The Indians exit singing and dancing. Then Christianity enters, dressed as a Spanish lady, with her escort Zeal, dressed as a captain in the Spanish army. Zeal responds to the Indian ritual in the typical style of the Spanish nobleman in the plays of the Golden Age. He wants to avenge the insult to Christianity, but Christianity is inclined to compassion and wants to persuade the Indians to adopt the Catholic religion. When Occident and America enter, they respond to Zeal's costume and weapons as the Indians had responded to their first visions of the Spanish army. The army attacks, driving the Indians from the stage, who surrender to force, but not to new beliefs. Then Christianity reasons with them about their god, explaining to them that the Eucharist is a continual sacrifice, embued with all the powers of flesh and blood victims but without the violence. The *loa* ends with a transition into the *auto sacramental*, which further dramatises the power of the Eucharist.

Sor Juana died of the plague in 1691. She was published in her lifetime in Spain and her *Reply* was published in 1700, in the third volume of her collected works. A recent edition of the complete works of Sor Juana has been published in Spanish. Unfortunately, only *The Reply* has been translated into English. There is, however, renewed interest in Sor Juana. Octavio Paz has completed a full study of her life and works (in Spanish) entitled *Sor Juana Inés de la Cruz o las trampas de la fé*, and Estela Portillo Trambley has written a play on her life (bilingual edition) entitled *Sor Juana*.[11]

Mercy Warren

In 1773, Mrs Mercy Otis Warren, the first American woman playwright, began writing plays in support of American revolutionaries. (The use of the term 'American' is both necessary and convenient in this section, primarily because what little literature exists regarding Warren's work uses that terminology; the author recognises that, technically, the term is imprecise and misleading.) She started writing at the age of forty-four, never having seen a play on the stage. Her goal was to 'strip the Vizard from the Crafty', or to attack the wealthy oligarchs who represented British royal interests against the republican values of the revolution.[12] Her first play, *The Adulateur* (1773), was inspired by a request from John Adams that she write a play on the theme of the Boston massacre. The play is in the five-act, blank-verse form with an all-male cast. The Boston patriots are given Roman names such as Brutus and Cassius, but the real heroes they represent are recognisably contemporary. The play was first published in a radical newspaper, *The Massachusetts Spy*, and later a revised version was published as a pamphlet.

Warren's next two plays were also for male casts and based on republican historical themes, so Abigail Adams asked her to write a play in which she remembered the ladies. She complied with *The Ladies of Castile* (1790). The heroine is a revolutionary leader named Maria, who organises a group of women to steal valuable relics from the Church in order to replenish the treasury of the revolutionaries – their task is both daring and dangerous. In this play, Warren not only depicts female revolutionaries: she even gives them dialogue about the incorrect views the male revolutionaries have of them. Maria explains the male prejudice against strong women in a dialogue with a male revolutionary. He is shocked by her activities and says, 'Hah! – durst thou venture on so bold a deed!' She replies, 'Necessity must sanctify the deed.' He then tells her,

> Thy soul was formed to animate the arm
> Of some illustrious, bold, heroic chief,
> And not to waste its glorious fire away,
> Beneath the weakness of the female form.

Maria retorts,

> Men rail at weaknesses themselves create
> And boldly stigmatize the female mind,
> As though kind nature's just impartial hand
> Had formed our features in a baser mould.

Maria then tells him she would explain more, but she must go –
she is too busy with revolutionary work for lengthy conversation
on this topic. In other words, she exits leaving the male
revolutionary standing idly about, musing on his own prejudices
about women.

There is no stage history for Warren's plays. They were not
written for the stage and have never enjoyed professional
production. In general, her plays are not included in anthologies
of American plays, nor in courses on American theatre. Moreover,
Warren has yet to emerge with the title of the first American
woman playwright. A feminist perspective on Warren does appear
in an unpublished dissertation by Louise Mason, 'The Fight to be
an American Woman and a Playwright' (University of California,
Berkeley, 1983), and in the article 'Mercy Warren, Satirist of the
Revolution' by Alice Robinson in *Women in American Theatre*.[13]
Nevertheless, Warren, like Hrotsvit and Sor Juana, remains
invisible in traditional theatre history. The absence of these
women causes the suppression of the tradition of women
playwrights. The invisibility of their biographies suppresses
valuable knowledge about the experience and models of women
in theatre. Though 'firsts' seem to be important in dominant
histories, 'first women' do not.

The preceding discussion has been designed to provide a sample
of 'firsts': the first women playwrights, the first women to make
their living by writing for the stage, the first woman playwright in
the New World and the first in the United States. In some cases,
these 'firsts' have been constructed from scanty information and
critical conjecture. They are intended to provide suggestions for
areas of future research and writing by feminist historians and
critics, along with sample suggestions of how to interpret the
available information from a feminist perspective. This notion of

'firsts' is borrowed from traditional histories, which always privilege pioneers. As we have seen, that privilege is often the result of a cultural code which seeks to legitimise its perspective by establishing pioneers as paradigms. Hopefully, feminist histories will be able to avoid this elitist application. While it is vital to take note of the women who have created plays as traditionally understood, it is also important to discover other kinds of performances women have created which might be termed 'theatre' and which do not duplicate the values of the dominant tradition.

Chapter 3

Personal Theatre

Since women have generally been confined to the domestic domain and denied admittance to the public arena, their performance space has often been within their houses. Their focus has been directed to the personal networks of family and friends, creating kinds of experience which did not lend themselves to articulation in the public figures of rhetoric and oratory. For this reason, some women have developed a different tradition of dialogue from that of men. These women have excelled in the personal forms of dialogue: letters, in the sphere of written communication, and conversation, in that of oral. This personal dialogue is created by partners in production rather than by an absent author who designs it for production in front of a reading or listening audience. It is a dialogue built on mutuality and intersubjectivity, eliminating any sense of formal distance or representation. Personal dialogue is not removed from life, so it operates not by mimesis but by enactment. It is an engaged dialogue, rooted in everyday life, rather than a mimetic dialogue, aimed at lasting repetition. This is the dialogue of present time, caught up in the movement of history and development without the secure fourth wall of formal closure.

The salon

Traditionally, the theatre of this personal dialogue was the salon.[1] The audience was composed not of consumers who paid for admittance, of strangers who came to listen to the removed dialogue of the traditional theatre, but of personal friends and interesting acquaintances, who came specifically to engage in social dialogue with one another. The absent playwright and the passive audience member were replaced by numerous actors who created their own lines and listened to the original dialogue of the others. No one spoke alone and no one spoke for others. The women who ran the salons played all the parts involved in theatrical production: the playwright (in conversation), the director (in casting the production by creating the guest list, helping create the scenes by making the introductions, setting the pace by actively keeping the conversation going), the actor, the set-designer (in decorating the home, deciding the menu, choosing the room for the evening) and the costume-designer (in setting the fashion and formality of the dress code). Though the guests were co-producers in many of these functions, the hostess defined the parameters of the occasion.

However, selecting the salon to represent women's personal theatre once again raises the problem of elitism. The salon was primarily the province of privileged women – women privileged by money, breeding, beauty and access to powerful men. These were often the same women as are included in traditional histories. In order to focus on women who are less privileged, this section will be devoted to two *salonières* with attributes which made them outsiders to aristocratic privilege: Rahel Varnhagen and Natalie Barney – Rahel because she was a Jew in Berlin (outside the German aristocracy), relatively poor, unschooled and unattractive (in her own opinion and that of others), and Natalie Barney because she was a lesbian, who devoted many of her social events to the entertainment of homosexuals.

Rahel Varnhagen

Rahel Varnhagen's salon was a centre for Berlin cultural life from the 1790s to 1806. The daugher of a Jewish money-lender, Rahel was early accustomed to engaging in dinner conversation with acquaintances of many kinds. Jewish money-lenders were expected to transact their business in their homes, and Rahel's father had a mixed clientele of noblemen, actors scholars and writers. He regularly mixed business with pleasure, inviting his clients to stay for dinner and other social events. Rahel was raised amidst this heterogenous mixture of classes and religions. Her salon exhibited the same kind of heterogeneity: Gentile mixed with Jew and aristocrats with artists. This had a socio-political effect beyond her salon, leading to friendships and even marriages that cut across the prevailing cultural codes which segregated classes and religions. Rahel's personal theatre staged an alternative dialogue which the culture at large discouraged. Though some German plays of the period depict both the upper and lower classes, the dramatic action is usually one of conflict rather than integration. Rahel's personal theatre was a laboratory for social change.

Rahel's salon had a mixed cast of characters, but its topics of conversation were fairly regular. They included theatre, literature, theological questions, Italian composers, historical events and comparative political systems. These topics are rather disparate, but the matters discussed on any particular occasion depended on the company. Thus theatre was the topic when actors and theatre-goers were present. Composers played their new works and listened to the reaction of the guests. Writers read works in progress and revised them upon hearing listeners' remarks. In this way, even the formal, traditional arts became part of the personal, improvisatory dialogue. Rahel's salon personalised art at the same time as 'the late 18th-century philosophers began to espouse the disinterestedness of art, and poets to assert the autonomy of literature'. It was the time of 'Kant's "pulchritudo vaga" – a beauty independent of any particular or finite significance'. And it was the time of the rise of the Romantics, who 'tended to perpetuate this tendency for an autonomous art, one defined by aesthetic criteria alone'.[2] In other words, the dominant, patriarchal philosophy and art of the time were invested in an art that stood apart from life and remained separate from the concrete realities of daily living. Yet, when art moved to the domestic domain of women, its context and goals were radically altered. The personal became the aesthetic and everyday life replaced the universal and eternal.

Rahel sometimes led this dialogue by directing the conversation. While the topics were focused and the conversation sometimes led, it was not a goal-oriented activity. Rahel was more interested in encouraging improvisation and play. She once wrote, 'I will write you letters where the soul can take a stroll, and not a goal-oriented purposeful trip on well-trodden, dusty highways. We want to walk on fresh, small, abstract paths that we don't even know.'[3] While salon dialogue was generally self-conscious about style, wit and pertinence, Rahel's sense of the language led her to explore the interior monologue, seek to articulate the unsaid. For her, language was not a polished instrument, but the sounds which trailed behind her interaction with ideas and people. Her writing style has been described as one which 'erupts with misplaced relative pronouns; postplaced modifiers; awakward, unbalanced phrasing; asyndeton; faulty punctuation, spelling, diction; frequent intrusions of French'.[4] Perhaps this style was also produced by her lack of education and her financial and social restrictions. Or perhaps her inattention to style was evidence of her continual engagement in the present, her dedication to the open form: 'Language is not at my command, not German, not my own; our language is our lived life; I have invented mine myself.'[5] Rahel's use of language preceded the feminist experiment in an alternative 'women's discourse' which is described in Chapter 4. Rahel perceived her use of language and her sense of dialogue as different from the prevailing patriarchal discourse of her times, disrupting or ignoring the stylistic rules of public expression. Her collected letters stand as a central document in the study of the history and ideas of a woman's personal diction in her period.

The personal theatre of the salon was a theatre without assumed characters – people spoke their lines as themselves. Rahel's idea of 'self', or character, was very different from the one dominant at the time. In a letter, Rahel wrote to a friend that, if she were to lose him, she would lose a part of herself, because only he recognised that part and without his recognition it would die. Rahel didn't imagine herself as a whole self, complete, discrete and independent. She had a sense that her self could only exist in mutuality – through the perception and interaction of others. Rahel's self was constructed in social interchanges, just as her dialogue was. One need only contrast this sense of self with the idea of a 'complete' character, or, even more intensely, with the construction of a stock character. Rahel was not interested in anything like a 'through line' or a 'super-objective', for her self or anyone else's. Rahel's self, dialogue and scenarios were formed by their intersection in the present moment. Rahel's personal theatre was ahead of its time. As we shall see in later chapters, her self, or sense of character, was like the post-modern decentred subject. Her dialogue was like the improvisations of twentieth-century theatre and her creation of the social and aesthetic as personal foreshadowed the feminist slogan 'The personal is the political'.

Natalie Barney

In the twentieth century, Natalie Barney created another type of personal theatre, which included personal performances, tableaux, a salon and garden theatricals. Inter-subjectivity, domestic space and personal friends were the essential elements of Barney's theatre as they had been of Rahel Varnhagen's. In addition, Natalie Barney created a personal theatre of sexuality – specifically lesbian sexuality. The events were often staged exclusively by women for women, celebrating the sexuality among women. Though Barney's theatricals exhibited all of the privileges of her wealth, with elaborate costumes and famous guests, they also exhibited the way the dominant culture oppressed the expression of lesbian sexuality by confining it to such gardens and private places. The traditional canon of art, literature and theatre omits almost entirely any images of lesbian experience or sexuality. Barney's personal theatricals were some of the earliest expressions of a lesbian dramatic sensibility, which was not to find an outlet on the professional stage until the rise of feminist theatre in the 1970s.

Natalie Barney was a rich American, living in exile in Paris from around the turn of the century until her death in 1972, at the age of ninety-four. Most of the literature on Barney concentrates on her vast number of seductions and affairs. The titles of the two major works about her emphasise this part of her life: *The Amazon of letters: The Life and Loves of Natalie Barney* (which includes on the cover a photograph of Barney kissing another woman) and *Portrait of a Seductress*.[6] In a sense, Barney's seductions were performances in themselves. In a society in which any signs or symbols of lesbian attachment were taboo, Barney made her liaisons public. Her seductions were played out in romantic symbols, costumes, role-playing and scenarios, combined with calculated displays of lesbian affection and sexuality at social events. Barney exhibited her sexuality in an era when most women hid it. These performances, in making lesbianism culturally visible, are a key element in Barney's legacy. One such performance was Natalie's first public seduction in Paris: she chose the famous courtesan Liane de Pougy. Her choice was startling – Pougy was a symbol of successful illicit heterosexual liaisons. Barney's lesbian advances at social events challenged the exclusivity of heterosexuality. Barney and Pougy developed an exciting narrative of seduction, which reached its culmination after their desire had been consummated. They rode together in an open carriage through the Bois de Boulogne, with Barney, dressed as a page, sitting at Pougy's feet. Their public performances continued at operas and other events, scandalising Parisian society. In 1901 Pougy even published a novel based on this affair, entitled *Idylle saphique*. The role-playing and social scenarios became fixed in the narrative form. Both the tableau they performed in the Bois and Pougy's novel attest to the symbolism, the conscious role-playing and the sense of form which accompanied this affair. Though such displays exhibited an upper-class sense of 'radical chic', they were also displays of female sexuality which broke social codes, flaunting images denied by society. Barney's seductions were resistance pieces, played out in front of the mainstream, heterosexual society. Perhaps wealth and privilege allowed her to break sexual codes without the fears of violent retaliation she might have suffered had she belonged to another class. However, her disregard for taboos did ensure that she would never travel in the dominant salon society of Paris. Though her salon attracted many famous artists, they were primarily homosexuals. Natalie's personal theatre was a luxurious ghetto for homosexually identified people in the arts.

Barney extended her tableaux of lesbian sexuality to photographs. She and her friends posed for these photos in costumes or settings which displayed mythological metaphors for their relationships: for instance, 'nymph and shepherdess' in bucolic costumes, Barney and Romaine Brooks in drag from various periods, and Barney and Renée Vivien as page and lady. Without a literary or theatrical vocabulary for their attachments, Barney and her friends began to create scenes which suggested imagistic renderings of their experiences. The creation of tableaux has often provided a beginning for the theatrical enterprise. For example, tableaux in the medieval Church and Renaissance masques provided the origins of the theatre practice of their times. Barney's performances and tableaux soon became a source

Beyond the salon

Before proceeding to women in performance art, the notion of
personal theatre should be expanded to included women's
performance activities beyond those located in the relatively
privileged arena of salon life. Helen Krich Chinoy and Linda
Walsh Jenkins, in *Women in American Theatre*, emphasise
women's roles in performance events such as church theatricals,
parades and Native American tribal ceremonies. Political
performances could in themselves provide material for a complete
chapter, though the clear demarcation beween personal and
political would need to be revised. Chinoy and Jenkins include
such political performances as the Women's Crusade of 1873–4,
actions taken by the Women's Christian Temperance Union in its
fight against the consumption of alcohol, and activities of the
Women's Trade Union League and the National Women's Party.
By way of contrast, they also include in their tally of performance
events involving women beauty pageants such as the Miss America
contest and homecoming parades. The authors note that 'these
roles in performance have been women's rights . . . to create for
others, for community, for social and religious good. . . . Often
woman is herself a social decoration; even her self adornment is
done for the pleasure of others and might be understood as her
way of being a visual artist within sex role demands.'[9]

Chinoy and Jenkins link these activities to women in traditional
theatre. In the US theatre, they note, women have worked
primarily in the small regional or art theatres which provide the
alternative theatre tradition to Broadway. The authors suggest
that 'women seem to have found the sharing, collective, creative
community aspects of theatre especially congenial. They have
tended to commit their energies to the nurturing art rather than
to the competitive business of theatre.'[10] This notion of the
unique suitability or preference of women for 'the nurturing art'
has become influential among some feminists working in theatre
criticism as well as among many contemporary women performers.
The concept of 'nurturing' raises the issue of how to interpret
women's work in the domestic arena, or, more deeply, of how to
interpret the relationship between women and their biological
nature.

The inclusion of broad social, political and community work in the category of theatre creates new perspectives on women and performance that reverse patriarchal evaluations of such projects. It privileges women's work, re-evaluating 'amateur' theatricals within the parameters of personal, domestic and social action rather than in relation to the canon or Broadway. There are, however, several aspects to this way of thinking that have become major points of disagreement within feminist criticism. The concept of 'nurturing' raises crucial questions about the nature of gender. Some feminist critics argue that women are by nature 'nurturing', interested in bonding and uninterested in competition, while materialist feminists perceive this as 'biologism' – the transformation of socio-cultural determinants into the biology of gender. 'Nurturing' also suggests a kind of mothering capability, recalling the biological ability of women to have babies. The materialists would argue that this 'nurturing' behaviour has simply been induced by society to keep women out of the market place by romanticising their confinement to the domestic sphere. 'Nurturing' is an extension of that domestic, mothering role. Materialist feminists argue that to privilege this behaviour in women merely reifies their oppression.

This difference among feminist critics creates several options for interpreting the domestic, social-service projects of women, such as salons, children's theatre and church theatricals. If one assumes that the domestic, social-service sphere of women is a sign of their socio-economic oppression, created by patriarchal culture to subordinate women to men in the market place, then to include such performance events in the theatre history of women may help to reproduce a ghetto for women's talent – an appropriation of their labour. However, one can choose to privilege what the dominant culture has discarded, reversing the traditional values to construct the perspective of the oppressed. What women have created in those performance events articulates their experience and creates new forms. Unfortunately, to cast this in terms of 'nurturing' suggests that the history of women in performance may have something to do with their biological gender – their bodies. And yet the biologistic model has not only become influential in feminist criticism: it has become operational in contemporary feminist performances, particularly in performance art.

Judy Chicago's art exhibit 'Dinner Party' exemplifies some of these ideas. Chicago took the domestic woman's activity of the dinner party and made it an aesthetic metaphor for a collection of the achievements of women. Each setting represents a famous woman in myth or history. The setting is composed of a plate, silverware, a place mat, and so on. Each plate uses the image of the clitoris to give a sense of the woman it represents. For example, the plate for the Amazon has a steel-grey clitoris, hard and strong-appearing to suggest a warrior. Hundreds of women used their skills in weaving, embroidery and other crafts to produce this project, which has travelled to museums throughout the United States. 'Dinner Party' not only exhibits the formal influence of such biologistic thinking: its director, Judy Chicago, has been a leading influence in the creation of the genre of women in performance art.

Performance art

Performance art is a new form that encompasses many of the alternative practices of women in performance throughout history. Beginning with the women mimes of Greece and Rome, whose 'scripts' were inscribed on their bodies, and continuing through the personal, sexual salons of Varnhagen and Barney, a tradition has emerged of how women might perform within the parameters of their own unique experience. This tradition has finally produced its own, unique genre of women in performance art – a practical theatre tradition outside the dominant tradition of stages, characters, plots, written texts and even audiences. Women performance artists choose personal sites for their performances, often without audiences. They explore new relationships to their own bodies and voices in performance and they develop new kinds of plays. Moira Roth's book *The Amazing Decade* is the leading historical document of women's art performances in the 1970s.[11] She identifies women's performance art as primarily a West-coast movement in the United States, springing initially from the early workshops and other activities led by the artist Judy Chicago. Women in performance art began in the late 1960s with Chicago's work in Fresno, California, and in the early 1970s moved with her to Los Angeles, where her group and others founded Womanhouse. The house became a site for art installations and performances that drew on experiences of women, particularly in the context of the domestic sphere.

Suzanne Lacy is one of the earliest and best-known performers in the art. She worked with Judy Chicago in the early days and proceeded to create a number of performance-art pieces that dramatised central issues in the social feminist movement. Her pieces combine feminist activism with visual and verbal metaphors of intense internal experiences. In 1977 Lacy organised *Three Weeks in May*, a series of performance events around the issue of rape. For three weeks, rape reports were recorded on a 25-foot map in the City Hall shopping mall in Los Angeles. Women's support agencies were registered on another such map. In surrounding areas, various performance artists produced public and private pieces. Lacy created a concluding piece in which four nude, blood-stained women crouched on a ledge above the door of the performance space. When people entered the gallery, they encountered a suspended, fleeced lamb cadaver with wings, and a poem about assault, scratched in asphalt, and heard tapes of women describing their rape experience. *Three Weeks in May* initiated a new poetic of women's theatre in practice. The location of the dramatic action was in truth the city of Los Angeles. The maps were located in a space frequented by women – a shopping mall. Lacy's maps confronted hundreds of women – intersecting their personal shopping – with the objective facts about violent crimes against women committed in that city at that time. Lacy created a three-week dramatic focus on the issue of rape. Her own piece, derived from discussions with rape victims, enacted the victim's subjective internal experience of rape. The objective–subjective blend of the political and the personal created a theatre of feminist consciousness-raising.

Carolee Schneeman, like the women mimes of Greece and Rome, made her own body the site for her play in *Interior Scroll* (1975). Schneeman pulled the written text of the performance out of her vagina. The text related a male film-maker's critical statements about her art, focusing on elements commonly attributed to the female gender: 'the persistence of feelings', 'the Hand-touch sensibility', and so on. Schneeman's image both reified and ironised the sense that there is a direct relationship between the female body and the cultural attributes of the female gender. Since Schneeman performed nude, directly relating to

one of her sexual organs, her image could be viewed as powerfully
biologistic, if it is perceived as the text produced by one of the
female sexual organs. Schneeman could be interpreted as
performing Irigaray's concept of beginning with the body organ in
the production of female form. *Interior Scroll* also ironised the
birth/artistic-creation paradigm so familiar to the dominant culture
(the patriarchal appropriation of giving birth as an image of the
artist as creator). Finally, the performance could be interpreted
as acting out the patriarchal fiction of the female gender. The
male film-maker/viewer has inserted his perception of Schneeman in her vagina by his perception of her, which she extracts to
read.

Leslie Labowitz's *Sproutime* (1980) was like a performance-art
transformation of Natalie Barney's garden parties. Labowitz
performed the piece at her home in Venice, California. Audience
members, who were also her friends, entered her dark garage to
discover racks of germinating seeds from floor to ceiling and
Labowitz, nude, watering her plants. She read parts of a children's
book entitled *The Secret Garden*, then led them out into the
garden behind her house. The garden was filled with real and
artificial flowers, streamers, and so on, and the event concluded
with a sprout lunch for the guests. Labowitz used the image of
women's gardens and garden parties for her event. The work was
gender-specific in its performance: the book is a favourite of
young girls in the United States, and the garden lunch involved
women entertaining other women. In her book, Moira Roth
suggests that, politically, Labowitz might be performing the
necessary retreat and refreshment many women felt they needed
after a decade of political struggle – that perhaps it was also
necessary to provide alternative experiences to the violence
against women in the culture. Roth suggests that *Sproutime*
offered a viable moment of utopia away from violence on the
streets and in homes. Yet the event might be accused of exhibiting
the same kind of privilege that Barney's garden parties exhibited,
the privilege of leisure and retreat possible only for certain classes
of women. But, also like Barney's parties, it symbolised the sense
of oppression which could mandate a retreat. Both Schneeman's
and Labowitz's performances were personal theatre, but in
different modes. Schneeman's was personal to her own body,
actual words applied to her, while Labowitz performed in her

own private space, with friends. Both artists appeared in the nude – a vulnerable, open statement of the performer's body.

Other women performance artists totally break any sense of closure in performance by absorbing the performance into their daily lives. The performance does not occur at a specific time and place, but continuously, for long durations. In 1984, Linda Montano announced that she would live tied to her male friend by a rope for one year. Their performance was documented by photos of them walking down the street, living in their apartment, and so on. The performance was both external, available to those who saw it, and internal, in the changes the couple discovered within themselves by virtue of the experience. This implies that for the spectator, who saw only a small part of it, the piece was fragmented, the performance only suggestive, partial and ultimately internal to the performers. There was no defined performance space, no sense of the public gathering, no public speech or formal dialogue. The piece became a metaphor of 'couples' – the bond and bondage between a man and a woman. By its physical reality, it confronted the two with the situation in its most limited form, dramatising for the two of them 'the tie that binds'.

Women performance artists often develop their pieces from their own diaries. Diaries are commonly considered girls' books. In speaking the words of her diary, the performer performs herself, speaking in the most personal language of the self to the self. By thus performing her own life, she becomes the woman as subject, as her own self, in the public space of performance. The performer is woman as self, without the aesthetic distance of character. Vanalyne Green's *Trick or Drink* (1984) is an example of this tradition. From her diaries, early family snapshots and pictures from childhood books, Green dramatised the experience of growing up with alcoholic parents. From her later photos and diary entries she traced her adoption of addiction – from her teenage obsession with her weight, through compulsive eating and vomiting (bulimia), to becoming addicted to her lovers. Green ended the performance by moving into the audience and gazing at photos of her parents from later life back to early childhood – a kind of redemption process and requiem for lost lives. Her piece focused on the underlying problems of substance abuse, particularly the way social codes encourage the developing women to become addicted to food, to losing weight and to romantic attachments with men. The personal, vulnerable presence of the self as performer created an intimacy between the audience and the performer. The fourth wall of fiction had been torn away and the effect of the performance was intimate and specific. Though not engaged in conversation as in a salon, each audience member was implicated as a listener by Green's direct address and eye contact. In the end, she suggested no closure, did not hint that she was now healed, nor that the events were complete. Yet the piece was not a confession, but a performance of her internal growth.

While many performance-art pieces are gender-specific in their content, Rachel Rosenthal performs pieces which challenge the very notion of gender. In *The Arousing (Shock, Thunder)* (1979) Rosenthal removed head bandages to reveal a false beard, which she stroked and then tore off. Rosenthal said that the piece 'dealt with the fact that I had been male-identified for so long and that only through the women's movement did I realize suddenly I was a woman . . . the reason for that is because for so long, the idea of artist was that an artist was male; and I was an artist, therefore I must be male'.[12] In *Bonsoir, Dr Schön!* (1980) she demonstrated the way the culture had inscribed its codes on her body. She appeared nude (which for her was extremely painful) and the 'bad points' of her body were marked with red tape, rubber bats, spiders, and so on, by her female assistants. After dressing up in an acceptable public costume of suit and high heels, she described her relationship with her father – the encoding parent. In *Gaia, mon amour* (1983) she played a man, a woman, a clown and a mother goddess. She describes thus her pleasure in cross-gender role-playing in her work and life: 'I hate the kind of sexual role-playing that has gone on for so long. . . . I feel very androgynous. . . . I don't think of myself as female or male. . . . I wear these [camouflage] pants with a lot of earrings, you know. . . .'[13] Rosenthal's age makes all of this more striking and poignant – in her mid fifties, with a shaven head and using gestures that range from the male aggressive to the grandmotherly, her very presence and appearance challenge the notion of gender and its attendant modes of sexuality (including age).

This sample of women performance artists demonstrates the culmination of many of the themes and choices women in theatre have made throughout their history. To the degree that motifs from the past appear in contemporary practice, the elements of a tradition may be identified, illustrating that women in theatre may have established an alternative tradition to the standard history of men in theatre.

Chapter 4

Radical Feminism and Theatre

The previous chapters have utilised feminist theory and methodology to discover and describe the relationship between women and the history of the theatrical enterprise. The aim has been to illustrate the way feminist principles may be used to analyse historical figures. As we have seen, some of the women active before the feminist movement showed a concern for women's oppression and rights and helped pave the way for the exploration of women's issues in performance. This chapter and the two following will outline the direct influence of certain key feminist positions on the growth and development of theatre practice. Though the scope of this book allows for only a brief description of the different feminisms, readers who are interested in pursuing further research in this area may refer to Allison Jaggar's *Feminist Politics and Human Nature* for a full treatment of these ideas. Here the aim is to identify certain relationships between feminist political positions and actual plays and practices of the contemporary theatre, so as to enable readers to extend this sample method into their own research.

At the beginning of the feminist movement, the singular term 'feminism' was often employed to describe a variety of political and critical realms. This term was often interchangeable with the term 'the women's movement'. As feminist practice and thought developed in the 1970s, some women felt there was a critical distinction between those interested in 'women' in theatre and those interested in feminism and theatre. Feminism began to be perceived as a specific political practice and analysis, committed to radical change and direct political action. Some women began to distinguish between their interest in the work of women in the theatre and feminist politics. For example, the Women's Program of the American Theater Association perceives itself as not necessarily a feminist organisation, but as a programme dedicated to the study and practice of women in theatre.

As the 1970s progressed, 'feminism' gave way to 'feminisms'. Many distinct feminist positions emerged. A basic list might include radical feminism (sometimes called cultural feminism), liberal feminism, materialist feminism, socialist feminism, Marxist feminism, lesbian feminism, radical lesbian feminism, critical positions such as psychosemiotic feminist criticism, and *l'écriture feminine* (an application of French feminism). Since most feminisms declare themselves to be leaderless positions, without a central organisation or a 'party line', they do not necessarily represent discrete ideologies or political organisations. Though these positions have become clearly distinguished from one another, many feminists embrace a combination of them. The historical development of the movement has encouraged certain mixtures. For example, many women working in leftist policies in the 1960s came into the feminist movement with Marxist or ethnic political roots, combining a radical feminist position with a Marxist one. However, for the sake of clarity, these positions will be described as if they were discrete.

Radical feminism

Although the term 'radical feminism' continues to be used to denote a deep commitment to change (in the way that 'radical' is used in many political circles), it has also come to denote a specific set of ideas and practices. (The alternative appellation 'cultural feminism' is often used by materialist feminists to underscore the distance of this position from a materialist analysis. See Alice Echols's discussion 'The New Feminism of Yin and Yang' in *Powers of Desire*.) Since radical feminism is the predominant position in the United States, most of the examples of its influence on theatre practice will be drawn from there. Radical feminism is based on the belief that the patriarchy is the primary cause of the oppression of women. The patriarchy is the system which elevates men to positions of power through the notion of the *pater* or father, placing men in an economic and social executive position within the family unit, the market place and the state. The patriarchy represents all systems of male dominance and is regarded as the root of most social problems. In other words, the patriarchy has formed a male culture that wherever it has predominated has oppressed women of all socio-economic classes and races. The earlier chapters of this book demonstrate the influence of such radical feminist thought. The noun 'feminism' and the adjective 'feminist' are employed as if they denote single, clear definitions; the category of 'women' connotes that the experiences of all women may be subsumed within it; and the term 'patriarchy' emerges as a discrete ideology and practice that has predominated for most of Western history.

The radical-feminist emphasis on the patriarchy produced another major category of analysis and practice: the notion of a women's culture, different and separate from the patriarchal culture of men. Many radical feminists participate in this women's culture, a 'grass-roots movement concerned with providing feminist alternatives in literature, music, spirituality, health services, sexuality, employment and technology'.[1] They even contend that this women's culture has existed throughout history, from early matriarchal societies and cults of the various manifestations of the mother goddess, through covens of witches and women's guilds, to contemporary communities of believers and practitioners. This sense that women are essentially different from men has created a new vocabulary. For example, there are new spellings of the word 'women' that remove 'men' from the root (such as 'womon', 'womyn' and 'wimmin') and new formations of other words (such as 'herstory' for 'history'). These words are generally more prominent in radical-feminist language than the word 'feminist'. The emphasis placed on the patriarchy and women's culture make the notion of gender central to radical feminism. Patriarchal oppression is a gender oppression. The exclusivity of women's culture is an exclusivity of gender. Radical feminists focus much of their critical and practical work on identifying either male-gender oppression or female-gender strengths.

The early units of radical-feminist thought and practice,

women's consciousness-raising (or CR) groups, focused exclusively on the experiences, forms and practices of women. These groups were not organised along the lines of class, race or political commitment, but were open to all members of the gender 'woman'. The first task of CR groups was to provide women with a voice. After centuries of silence, CR groups provided a situation in which women could begin to articulate what it felt like to be a woman. The all-woman composition of the groups provided safety from the scrutiny and criticism of men and gave women an opportunity to enter into a dialogue with other women. They articulated their relationship to sexuality, the workplace and the family unit, as well as their dreams, memories, fantasies and hopes. These CR groups provided the beginning of feminist theatre, which celebrated the public performance of the voices of women, without questioning their condition or definition, class or colour. The first feminist theatre groups, such as the It's All Right to be Woman Theatre, reflected the CR composition and focus in their names. The first articles published on this subject reflect this same focus on women rather than feminism.[2]

The It's All Right to be Woman Theatre, founded in 1970, was one of the earliest feminist theatres in America. Its work provides a clear illustration of the effect of radical feminism on theatre practice. The name of the troupe suggests its position: to validate the experience of the category called 'woman'. The group used CR techniques along with movement and acting exercises to create its productions. These productions were a kind of public CR-group experience, heightened by a few theatrical techniques. In fact, they could be perceived as dramatisations of the dynamics of the CR process: the productions used material from the women's experiences that had emerged in the CR process, and the audience acted like a kind of extended CR group that listened to the individual member articulate her experience of being a woman. The emotional nature of the material and the sense of public exposure sometimes caused performances to be late or cancelled. Yet this same personal intensity also created a new kind of intimacy between audience and performer that broke with the traditional concept of the 'fourth wall', or aesthetic distance. This produced a new dramaturgical dynamic that matched the feminist sense that the personal is political. Moreover, the assumption of a commonality of women's experiences and the gender-specific nature of CR groups led this troupe and many others to the practice of performing to all-women audiences. They discovered that the relationship to an audience composed entirely of women was significantly different from the relationship that occurred when men were present.[3] Historically, feminist theatre has constituted a contradiction to the all-male composition of classical theatre, provoking a break with the codes of the dominant culture.

One of the major discoveries of radical feminism that raised women's consciousness of their experiences was that the oppression of women was a sexual, erotic oppression. Male culture made women's bodies into objects of male desire, converting them into sites of beauty and sexuality for men to gaze upon. Women learned to view their own bodies in the same way, and so were prevented from identifying with their own appearance. The It's All Right to be Woman Theatre opened its productions with a woman touching various parts of her body, reclaiming them from patriarchal colonisation. The troupe and audience would chant, 'our faces belong to our bodies, our bodies belong to our lives'. In the social movement, rituals such as bra-burnings also represented women reclaiming their bodies from the sexualising elements of patriarchal culture. It's All Right to be Woman used the materials from these demonstrations to create its production entitled *Sags and Supports*, dramatising the relationship between developing as a woman and wearing a bra. The early movement also extended this critique to the patriarchal appropriation of women's bodies as beautiful objects. In 1970 and 1971, there were demonstrations in London against the Miss World contest. Similar protests and theatricals were staged in the United States against the Miss America contest. The London protests included theatrical demonstrations such as *Sugar and Spice* (1971) by the Women's Street Theatre Group, whose props included a huge deodorant and a giant penis.[4]

However, the early movement also underscored the enforcement of the objectification of women's bodies by the institution of rape. Rape began to be perceived as the patriarchal weapon that directly wounded or violated women and indirectly, as a threat, kept women off the streets and alienated them from the expression of their own sexual desires. This new consciousness of rape as a social, patriarchal weapon rather than the perverse action of individual men produced a widespread influence on the theatre. The feminist theatre in Minnesota called At the Foot of the Mountain entitled its first production *Raped* (1976). The play was an adaptation of Brecht's *The Exception and the Rule*, interrupting Brecht's text with commentaries, based on the accounts of actual victims, on the experience of rape. The theatre's publicity described rape as 'about the most common form of world-wide oppression'. In this production, the radical-feminist critique of patriarchal, sexual-gender oppression intersected Brecht's Marxist critique of economic-class oppression. Nell Dunn's *Steaming* (1981) dramatises in the story of Dawn, who was raped by a police officer in the station where she worked, the psychological damage inflicted on the victim by rape. Dunn shows how rape creates fear and anger and contributes to mental instability. Ntozake Shange addresses the rage of the rape victim in *Three Pieces*, and explores its other effects in a story in *for colored girls who have considered suicide when the rainbow is enuf* (1970). *Rape-In* (1971) is a series of four plays by the Westbeth Feminist Collective of Connecticut, investigating rape as a literal and metaphorical oppression of women. *Pig in a Blanket* (1972), the first play by a feminist theatre in Minneapolis called Alive and Trucking, dramatises a gang rape.

Along with a new consciousness of women's sexual-gender oppression came a new consciousness of women's sexual rights. The right to safe, legal abortions became a central issue in the movement. One of the earliest plays on this subject was Myrna Lamb's *What Have You Done for Me Lately* (1969). This play was the first production of the New York Feminist Theatre, staged as a benefit for Red Stockings, a radical-feminist organisation. The play concerns the problems and fears of a man who wakes up to discover that he has been implanted with a pregnant uterus, without the choice of abortion. Lamb's play, along with many others, also brought the biological and sexual experiences of women to the stage. Women's bodies and biological experiences became dramatically visible in the new perspectives of feminism and women playwrights. Experiences that had never before been staged began to appear in the texts. A familiar example is Wendy Wasserstein's *Uncommon Women and Others* (1970). Women openly discuss the experience of menstruation, exhibiting a freer sense of exploration about their periods, including the tasting of one's own menstrual blood (i.viii).

The celebration of women's biological gender led some radical feminists to ally biology with certain mental and spiritual states. They asserted that women's menstrual cycles and child-bearing experiences brought them closer to nature than men. If women had not been famous thinkers, critics and philosophers, it was because they were more intuitive, or more spiritual. These biological characteristics were common to women of all ages, creating a common bond for women throughout history. *O Women's Piece* (1976) by the Rhode Island Feminist Theatre opens with an Amazon crawling toward the audience like an aroused jungle cat. She picks up a shield and a double axe, drops to her knees and looses a primal scream. This image resonates through the popular women's culture of radical feminists, many of whom wear the double axe around their neck as a symbol of the Amazon and of female spirituality. The opening scene of *O Women's Piece* signals the primal scream of all women, echoing through the ages and evoking the spiritual and intuitive powers of the women in the audience.

In spite of the sense of a transcendental bond among women, radical feminism focuses on the experiences of individual women. Women are not represented as members of a class or race, but as people with individual rights. The individual woman has a right to her own body and her own free will. An individual woman can do something about her life: she can burn her bra, rejecting the restrictive image applied to women's bodies, or she can take martial-arts classes to learn to resist violence against her body. As an actor, she can find her own female voice and break her own silence. Likewise, feminist theatre production primarily influenced by the discoveries of radical feminism are based on the stories, experiences or fantasies of individual women. Early productions dramatise the experiences of individual members of the troupe, or act out the stories of individual women in the community. The prominence of the individual and the rights of individuals allies radical feminism with the liberal-democratic tradition and distances it from the Marxist focus on the collective.

Though most feminist theatre companies have been organised as collectives, the collective status of the groups has more to do with a break with patriarchal organisations of power than with a break from individualism. The collective structure enhances the sense of women supporting other women and sharing their resources, but it has not informed the representation of women on stage. In the past decade, numerous studies of feminist theatre have appeared that document the organisational structures, development and productions of the troupes.[5]

Witches, goddesses and rituals

Radical feminism has created a women's culture as an alternative to the dominant, patriarchal one, and that culture has created its own performance events outside traditional theatre. These are grass-root, community rituals that dramatise the unique powers and experiences of women among women. The performers often live in a separatist or limited separatist environment. They are women who work in alternative woman-owned, operated and consumed businesses or trades, women who live in feminist collectives, women who live in lesbian-feminist separatist communities, or women who may work within the dominant culture but spend their leisure time in a separatist environment. Some of these performers are involved in goddess worship, some identify themselves as witches and many perform in a combination of goddess rituals and the rituals of witches. Within the radical-feminist tradition, their rituals compound women's intimate relationship with nature (particularly the bond between women's biology and nature) with such social issues as rape. The rituals commonly celebrate women's biological cycles, intuition, receptivity, fertility, bonding and nurturing. They cast the experiences and qualities of women in a spiritual arena rather than in the context of socio-political history. In this spiritual arena, women are depicted as the strong rather than the oppressed.

Two books by Mary Daly have been definitive in the construction of the radical feminist sense of spirituality: *Beyond God the Father: Toward a Philosophy of Women's Liberation* and *Gyn/Ecology: the Metaethics of Radical Feminism*. These books deconstruct and appropriate the symbols, metaphors, rituals, organisations and experiences of the patriarchal religions that have historically dominated the spiritual realm, with their male priests and their male gods. Daly suggests that women can discover their own spirituality through a new female language, creating their own symbols and events. According to Daly, women's way of perceiving, thinking and being is essentially different from men's and needs to be recognised outside the male systems of rationality, linear thought and hierarchical forms of spirituality. 'Spinsters spin and weave, mending and creating unity of consciousness. In doing so we spin through and beyond the multiple split of consciousness. In concealed workshops, Spinsters unsnarl, unknot, untie, unweave. We knit, knot, interlace, entwine, whirl and twirl.'[6] Daly's title *Gyn/Ecology* demonstrates the new language, with its gynocentric base and its inherent tie between women's biology and natural forces.

Susan Griffin is the other author who is central to a radical-feminist spirituality. The titles of two of her books, *Women and Nature: The Roaring inside Her* and *Rape/The Power of Consciousness*, illustrate the tie between women's biological, spiritual selves and the social issues of rape. Griffin voices the intimate bond between women and nature in this way, highlighting the privileged position of the female gender: 'We know ourselves to be made from this earth. We know this earth is made from our bodies. For we see ourselves. And we are nature. We are nature seeing nature. We are nature with a concept of nature. Nature weeping. Nature speaking of nature to nature.'[7]

Faminist witches' covens and goddess-worshippers incorporate the ideas of Daly and Griffin into their practice. They are Daly's 'concealed workshops' of 'Spinsters', acting out Griffin's sense of women and nature, combined with rituals around social issues. This new mixture of witches' covens and feminist politics is expressed in the name of one founded by Z. Budapest in Los Angeles in 1971 – the Susan B. Anthony Coven. Its manifesto declares that the members have 'the right to control our bodies' and 'our sweet womon souls', by 'defending our interests and those of our sisters through the knowledge of witchcraft' and through 'Goddess-consciousness'.[8] These covens perceive their organisation as an alternative to hierarchical structures; without central authorities determining their liturgy or rites, they are free to create their own rituals and chants.[9] Within these covens, the individual is prime: 'The self, one's individuality and unique way of being in the world, is highly valued.'[10]

Their rituals testify to the influence of radical feminism in their concentration on women's biological powers. For example, one way to prepare a wand is to 'dig out a little from one end and stuff it with a piece of cotton and a drop of your menstrual blood'.[11] A number of rituals celebrate the beginning of menstruation for young girls and the spiritual powers of the menstrual cycle. Hallie Iglehart and Barbry My Own performed a ritual that combined the celebration of the summer solstice with the experiences of menstruation and birth.

> The women simulated a birth canal and birthed each other into their circle. They raised power by placing their hands on each other's bellies and chanting together. Finally they marked each other's faces with rich, dark menstrual blood saying 'This is the blood that promises renewal. This is the blood that promises sustenance. This is the blood that promises life.' From hidden, dirty secret to symbol of the life power of the Goddess, women's blood has come full circle.[12]

The productions of some feminist theatre groups also illustrate the influence of these ideas. For example, *Lydia E. Pinkham's Menstrual Show* (1979), performed by the Actor's Sorority Theatre in Kansas City, Missouri, celebrated, says Curb, 'the magic of blood without violence'. In a humorous vein, *The Period Piece* (1980), produced by the Mischief Mime Company in Ithaca, New York, dramatised the relationship between a uterus and a tampon.

Feminist witches and goddess-worshippers also create rituals around the pain of patriarchal oppression, particularly the pain of rape. These rituals can either help the victim regain her inner strength or hex the rapists. In June 1980, many women gathered at the top of Mount Tamalpais, outside San Francisco. The mountain, formerly held sacred by Native Americans, had been the site of the murder of a woman the previous spring and of several rapes over the years. The ritual began with women standing in a circle and chanting,

> We are here to remember our sisters who have died on this mountain.
> We are here to remember that although we have been compared to this Earth,
> We are not allowed to walk it in safety,
> And we are not allowed to walk it alone.

The women send their pain and anger into the Earth, asking
that it be changed into energy for action; they invoke women
of the past, the ancient queens, priestesses of the Goddess, the
healers, the women burned as Witches, the women who tended
the land, all women past and present who have been oppressed
and have fought back. They chant again and again, 'I am a
woman, my Will is unbending', sending the words and their
energy out in webs to surround and reclaim the mountain.[13]

Z. Budapest describes a ritual to hex a rapist:

At the waning moon, take a black penis candle and write on it
what you want to happen to the rapist, anoint it with Double-
Cross oil and urine, placed on the altar before the image of the
Mother Goddess. Light incense, chant to Hecate, imagine what
could happen to the rapist as the candle burns, knowing that
'Rape is the foundation for patriarchy.'[14]

At the end of the ritual, the celebrant collects all the remnants of
the ritual and casts them into the waves, turning her back on
them.

The special relationship between women and nature is often
celebrated in rituals that concern cycles. Nature's solstices,
women's menstrual cycles, the cycles of the moon and the cycle
of life and death all combine to provide the union between
woman and nature. Rituals for the Spring Equinox recall Demeter
and Persephone as a mother–daughter myth, placing the earth's
seasons within a generational female relationship. Z. Budapest's
ritual prescribes that women kiss one another on the forehead,
eyes, lips, breasts and genitals, signifying the biological bond of
women, while Demeter recites a poem identifying parts of the
earth with the parts of her body. The cyclic celebrations of
witches are reflected in several feminist theatres. The New Cycle
Theatre in Brooklyn (founded in 1977) states that it takes its
name from the cycles of the female body, the seasons, the phases
of the moon, and birth and rebirth. Several of its productions
have been based on spiritual–mythological themes. For instance,
A Monster Has Stolen the Sun (1981), by Karen Malpede, includes
elements similar to those found in feminist rituals: a Celtic tribe,

an invocation to the sun and a child entering through a cervex-like opening in the scenery, connoting birth.

The New Cycle Theatre also exhibits the radical-feminist blend of biological spirituality with social commitment. In the case of this theatre, the commitment is to world peace. Malpede's *Making Peace: A Fantasy* (1979) is an example of this combination. In her book *Women in Theatre: Compassion and Hope*, she describes the play thus: 'The flowing of blood and of milk, the turning of blood into milk, renewable ecstasies – these are commonplaces of female sexuality. In this play, female sexuality works miracles. The play is a celebration of female sexuality.'[15] In other words, the powers inherent in women's biology and sexuality are capable of solving social ills. This is reminiscent of a witches' ritual of the full moon in which the moon is seen as 'a womb burgeoning with life', a 'sexual woman', inviting you to feel the 'power in your own pleasure, in orgasm'.[16] Another feminist group that has taken its name from the notion of cycles is the Circle of the Witch (founded in 1973) in Minneapolis. The name combines 'circle', 'a female symbol of roundness, eggs, ovaries, and a universal symbol of communication and cooperation', and 'witch', 'our link with a matriarchal past'.[17]

In Search of the Hammer (unpublished, 1983), written by Cappy Kotz and Phrin and produced by the Front Room Theatre in Seattle, offers an example of how the ideas, practices and lives of feminist witches have been integrated into a feminist play. The play opens in a women's bar, where the women hear that an archaeological dig has unearthed a hammer (the double axe) that is imbued with the power of the matriarchy. However, President Reagan and his men have taken possession of the hammer and have declared that it is a symbol of male power. Three of the women set out in search of the hammer. On their journey, they come to the Labia house, a large lavender house where a separatist community of spiritual women lives. Upon their arrival, the three discover the women performing a ritual to recover the hammer. They all join together in the search. When they find the hammer, their cunning, along with the magic power of the hammer, frees it from Reagan's men and magically transports them all back to the women's bar. The play ends with a ceremony of dancing and singing, which celebrates women taking back their power from the patriarchy. The play's setting, plot, characters and themes all testify to the influence of radical-feminist ideas: the combination of spirituality and social commitment, separatism, the oppression of the patriarchy, identification with earlier women's communities of Amazons and goddess-worshippers, the potency of rituals and the potential for individual women to take back the power the patriarchy has appropriated from them.

The radical-feminist perspective on witches extends beyond contemporary feminist witches to a re-vision of the representations and realities of witches from earlier historical periods. The witch hunts in England and the United States are reinterpreted as misogynistic massacres of women. The patriarchal persecution of the witch embodies a fear of women's sexuality, a repression of women's alternative healing-practices, the abolition of abortion, the rejection of women who choose to live a single life and the prohibition of women's communities. The witches themselves are represented as healers, herbalists, poor women who practised healing in order to maintain financial independence, single women and women who prefer the company of other women to the male-dominated associations of the dominant culture.

Many plays reflect this re-vision of witches, but perhaps the most familiar example is Caryl Churchill's *Vinegar Tom* (1976), co-created and produced by the Monstrous Regiment in London. The name of this feminist theatre is derived from a misogynist Puritan sermon delivered in the era of witch-burnings. In its class analysis, the play incorporates some elements of a feminist materialist analysis along with those of radical feminism. Set in seventeenth-century England, *Vinegar Tom* depicts the lives of several women who are ultimately hung as witches. The women are depicted not as witches, but as women who threaten the patriarchal class system in various ways. It is simply useful to destroy them. The songs in the play are delivered in a modern manner, suggesting that times may not be that different. In other words, the historical representation of witches actually represents the misogyny of the patriarchy.

Mary Beth Edelson, known as a performance artist of spiritual events, created a piece entitled *Proposals for: Memorials to 9000 Women Burned as Witches in the Christian Era* (1977). Edelson created a stark environment. On the walls she displayed enlarged photographs of rituals from a Neolithic cave; on the floor was a circle of stone-like handmade books representing the books of magic, and in the centre of the circle was an 11-foot high ladder – women were tied to ladders in the bonfires where they were burned as witches. The ladder stood for that practice as well as for women's spirituality – their ability to rise above persecution. The participants chanted the names of thousands of women who had been burned as witches. The performance was both a reminder and a warning to the women who participated.[18]

The radical-feminist focus on witches foregrounds both gender oppression and gender strength. The image of the witch provides a model of women-identified women who are in harmony with nature, or the order of things, rather than outsiders excluded from the dominant culture. The feminist witch creates a new tradition of women's performance as well as a tie to the history of such performances. These rituals empower the women who participate in them and reverse a central negative image of women into a positive one. Many of these same considerations have also created the radical-feminist focus on the lesbian and on lesbian theatre.

The lesbian and the theatre

The critique óf the patriarchal oppression of women by sexual means is sometimes extended to a critique of what Adrienne Rich has termed 'compulsory heterosexuality'. In what has become a central lesbian document within radical feminism, 'Compulsory Heterosexuality and Lesbian Existence',[19] Rich describes the 'institution of heterosexuality as a beach head of male dominance'. Rich identifies two ways in which heterosexuality is made compulsory: through 'the constraints and sanctions that, historically, have enforced or ensured the coupling of women with men' and, in a phrase she borrowed from Catherine MacKinnon, 'the eroticization of women's subordination'. The contradiction to compulsory heterosexuality is lesbian existence. Rich places lesbianism in the context of patriarchal oppression rather than in the bi-gender context of homosexuality. The lesbian, she suggests, performs an act of resistance to the patriarchal assumption that men have the right of access to women. Within radical feminism, the lesbian is a woman-identified woman because her primary relationships are with women, while the heterosexual woman is male-identified because she privileges her relationships with men. 'Heterosexuality separates women from each other; it makes women define themselves through men; it forces women to compete against each other for men and the privilege that comes through men and their social standing.'[20] In the early days of the movement, the lesbian critique became so sharp that it was often represented by this sentence attributed to Ti-Grace Atkinson: 'Feminism is the theory; Lesbianism is the practice.'

Like the witch, the lesbian experiences both the height of patriarchal misogyny and the height of female power. She invokes the hatred of men, who often regard her as 'not a woman'. She has been the victim of job discrimination, social discrimination and psychological discrimination because of her sexual preference for women. The lesbian refuses to be the sexual object of male desire while daring to appropriate his sexual territory. On the other hand, the lesbian can remain outside of the internal dynamics of patriarchal sexuality. She is independent from the legal and economic dependencies of heterosexual marriage and has access to the intimate support of other women. The lesbian is empowered by the woman-identified culture. One wing of this position became separatists, maintaining that the feminist social experiment could not take place within the patriarchy. This separatism sometimes included the rejection of heterosexual women.

As this critique spread, theatres were organised that were specifically for, by and about lesbians – many played only to all-women audiences. In this way, the theatres themselves became separatist institutions. New plays were written that emphasised the lesbian lifestyle and critique. Generally, these productions were aimed at dramatising positive images of lesbians. Lesbian theatre women in this tradition criticised the images of lesbians in mainstream plays such as *The Children's Hour* by Lillian Hellman because they presented lesbianism as a painful, defeating experience and because the lesbian relationship occurred not within a lesbian community, but within a heterosexual one.

Several lesbian theatres were created in the 1970s. Among these were the Lavender Cellar Theatre, founded in Minneapolis in 1973, which produced several plays, including *Prisons*, concerning lesbian activities in women's prisons, and *Cory*, a traditional 'coming-out' narrative; Medusa's Revenge, a group founded in New York in 1976, which produced *Bayou*, a musical fantasy about a lesbian bar, with dancing, torch songs, and so on; and the Red Dyke Theatre, founded in Atlanta, Georgia, in 1974, which produced satirical skits and dramatical sketches. Many such theatres operated for only a few years. While many have closed, many others have recently opened. Because these theatres are often under-funded, focus on a limited local audience and are not able to attract mainstream critics or publications, research in this area is difficult. The critic must rely on the theatre's own pamphlets, reviews in alternative periodicals and word of mouth.

A number of the plays developed for these theatres have been recently published in the first anthology of lesbian plays entitled *Places, Please!*[21] Two of these plays have been produced at several theatres across the United States: *Dos Lesbos* by Terry Baum and Carolyn Myers and *8×10 Glossy* by Sarah Dreher. *Dos Lesbos* follows a revue format, offering coming-out scenes in the manner of realism, Greek tragedy and Restoration comedy, songs about being a 'dyke', such as 'Misery Loves Company', and scenes about lesbians in the workplace and lesbian attitudes toward men. On the whole, *Dos Lesbos* has a light, 'campy' tone that captures the language of the 'bar dyke' culture of San Francisco. In contrast, *8×10 Glossy* is a realistic play about the problems between a lesbian and her family. Set in a rural, heterosexual environment, the lesbian character is isolated and alienated from her surroundings. This volume represents the first publication of underground plays that have been produced in amateur or alternative theatres. Most of the plays included in the volume are the first publication for their authors.

By contrast, Jane Chambers is a lesbian playwright whose plays have enjoyed many productions and publications. Though her plays are not strictly within the radical-feminist tradition, they offer many insights into the lesbian theatrical perspective. *Last Summer at Blue Fish Cove* (1982), one of Chambers's most popular plays, dramatises the interaction between the regulars in a lesbian-summer-resort community and a heterosexual woman who unknowingly rents one of the cabins. The play is a mixture of melodrama and comedy. Some of the humour is based on the uneasiness of the lesbians around the heterosexual woman – particularly one, a famous author of books on sexuality, who is 'in the closet'. Other humorous incidents are based on the heterosexual's complete dependence on her former husband for her knowledge of her own sexuality, and her naïveté about other people and practical matters because of the privilege of heterosexual marriage, which has both protected her from some experiences and denied her others. By the end of the play, she has fallen in love with one of the lesbians and will set out on a life of freedom and independence for herself. In this play, the lesbian community is the norm and the heterosexual is the outsider. Her presence is felt as a potential menace and the occasion of social unease. The heterosexual woman is also the stereotype. These elements create a lesbian perspective, inverting the dramatic conditions of mainstream plays that portray the lesbian as the outsider, the stereotype and the social menace.

The play also depicts the mutual sharing of domestic labour in lesbian relationships, and the creation of a kind of surrogate family. It portrays a gamut of lesbian lives and relationships, rather than portraying one lesbian in isolation, or as a 'type'. One lesbian is a mother, two play the traditional roles of 'butch' and 'femme', some are rich and some without means. Though the play falls within radical feminism in its organisation of the lesbian point of view and its critique of heterosexuality, it is not really a lesbian-feminist play. In fact, Kitty, the famous author 'in the closet', is the only character who introduces feminist ideas. Feminist concerns are distanced from the play, seemingly intellectual abstractions in contrast to lesbians' daily lives.

Chambers's last play, *Quintessential Image* (1983), dramatises the dialectic between the reality of lesbian experience and the social perception of the lesbian. The setting is a television talk show, a metaphor for the social presentation of the self determined by the dominant codes of representation. The cameramen represent the codes, censoring and reifying whatever images they choose to broadcast. The audience watches the television images on monitors and the live action on the stage, aware of the concurrences and contradictions between real experiences and representations. The show's famous guest is a photographer, who 'comes out' as a lesbian on camera. She points out that most of her famous photos were inept attempts to photograph the woman she loved, or something important to that woman. Instead, by coincidence and error, she photographed important events in the history of the dominant culture, obscuring the view of the woman she loved and making herself famous as a photographer. The photos are hung in the National Gallery because they are perceived as pictures of men and their history, while the woman remains a blur. The talk-show hostess becomes increasingly nervous during these public disclosures. She and the cameramen attempt to select something presentable to broadcast. The cameras shoot wildly around the studio and the hostess repeatedly tries to interrupt and cover up the photographer's revelations, rather like the famous men who conceal the woman in the photos. The highpoint of the situation occurs when the photographer asks the hostess when she will 'come out of the closet'. She had discovered the hostess was a lesbian in a conversation with a friend at a women's bar.

The dramatic tension of the play is focused on the nature of socially acceptable images. Lesbian experience has been made invisible by men and their history. The photographer, now photographed, foregrounds the lesbian and challenges the sign system of the dominant culture. She centres representation on the lesbian, moving her image from the margin to the centre. Ironically, the talk-show hostess, queen of dominant images, is revealed as an invisible lesbian, who has sacrificed her own representation. The play exposes compulsory heterosexuality in its control of culture. The men who control the television cameras continue to obscure the concerns of the lesbian photographer. Yet the audience perceives the contradiction between compulsory heterosexuality and lesbian existence.

Interest in the representation of the lesbian on stage has led some women to explore the situation of the lesbian actor. As noted above, the male gaze perceives the lesbian as 'not a woman' – she does not adjust her image to attract the male gaze. In this way, the lesbian challenges the social constructions of gender in her appearance. She is estranged from both masculine and feminine costumes and gestures. The French critic Monique Wittig has written an influential article on this subject entitled 'One is not Born a Woman'. In it, she reveals the political motivation for the construction of gender, valorising the lesbian as the only one who can escape the trap of gender.

Wittig and Sande Zeig have become pioneers in presenting the non-gendered lesbian actor on stage. Zeig toured in Wittig's play

The Constant Journey (1984), about a female Don Quixote. Feminist critics have celebrated Zeig's performance as an exceptional blend of masculine and feminine gestures, or as beyond such gestures. As Harriet Ellenberger notes in an article on lesbian theatre, 'According to Sande Zeig, the gestures appropriate to women are the gestures of slaves. It follows, I suppose, that the gesture appropriate to men are the gestures of slavemasters. Neither is appropriate to a free human.'[22] Ellenberger goes on to describe Zeig's performance as 'a little butch, a little femme, a little childhood ambition, a little cross-species dressing (a detachable fur tail, for instance, gives one a lovely feeling); mix and match, stalk and slink, strut and flutter.'

Zeig and Wittig have extended this work into acting and movement classes. In 1984, they offered a class in 'Dynamics of Language and the Semiotics of Gesture' at New York University. They experimented with 'a series of techniques specifically designed for learning the other sex class gesture system'. They encouraged the students to discover their own 'impersonator' – 'an impersonator is not a character that one constructs out of fictional information. An impersonator is oneself, but as the opposite sex.'[23] Work on the impersonator was used to help the students identify the movements of both sex classes as well as their own personal movement pattern. The students watched video tapes of their own work, studied photographs of gendered gestures and observed subjects on the street.

From this work, Zeig and Wittig hope to deconstruct the gestures of gender. They hope to discover a way for actors to become aware of social gender movement and to distance themselves from that movement pattern. Specifically, they see this as the work of the lesbian actor: 'lesbians' task is to change the form of the actors' movement and gestures . . . through gestures, lesbians are able to radically influence the direction of contemporary theatre'.[24]

A new generation of lesbian critics have started to create what they hope will become a new lesbian theatre aesthetic. Using plays that embody the lesbian perspective, Wittig and Zeig's new lesbian acting-style, as well as elements of traditional acting-theory, they seek to articulate a lesbian dramaturgy. Jill Dolan has begun to develop an analysis, working with the notion that the fundamental elements of traditional drama are difference and conflict. According to Dolan, traditional drama is based on the concept of oppositional genders.[25] Playing with such cultural idioms as 'opposites attract', traditional texts exhibit a form that depends on the resolution of differences or the creation of alliances between opposites, such as the convention of ending plays with the institution of heterosexual marriage, a device which combines the oppositional mode with the enforcement of compulsory heterosexuality. Dolan notes that this aesthetic is not suitable to a single-gender, or homosexual, experience. The questions Dolan raises could lead to a new aesthetic. What would theatre be like if it were distanced from cultural oppositions? What kind of form would result from a focus on similarity? What could constitute dramatic action outside of conflict? What could constitute character outside of cultural gender? Dolan's questions about a lesbian aesthetic could prove to be central to any notion of feminist theatre.

Chapter 5

Materialist Feminism and Theatre

The term 'materialist feminism' is used here as an umbrella to cover the common elements of several positions, but primarily those of Marxist feminism and socialist feminism. Though there are important differences among these positions, for the purpose of this book their common base in historical materialism will serve to distinguish them from other feminisms. The perspective of historical materialism directly contradicts the essentialism and universalism of radical feminism. Rather than assuming that the experiences of women are induced by gender oppression from men or that liberation can be brought about by virtue of women's unique gender strengths, that patriarchy is everywhere and always the same and that all women are 'sisters', the materialist position underscores the role of class and history in creating the oppression of women. From a materialist perspective, women's experiences cannot be understood outside of their specific historical context, which includes a specific type of economic organisation and specific developments in national history and political organisation. Contemporary women's experiences are influenced by high capitalism, national politics and workers' organisations such as unions and collectives.

Derived from Marxism, materialist feminism posits that class determines the situation of all people within capitalism. The dynamics of class consciousness are central in the formation of all economic, social and cultural institutions. Class biases determine the attitudes of individuals in the spheres of labour, interpersonal relationships and the production of cultural artefacts. This assumption implies that works of art reflect the class of the artist and that bonds between people are usually the bonds of a shared class. Class is a hierarchical structure in which the owners of the means of production garner their privileges through the oppression of the workers. The definitive role that class plays in social organisation means that there are crucial differences between upper-middle-class women and working-class women – not only are all women not sisters, but women in the privileged class actually oppress women in the working class.

The primacy of socio-economic factors focuses this critique on the spheres of labour and production. Production is the central human action played out in the market place and, for women, in the domestic sphere. The organisation of the forces of production and the role of wages create the situation of the worker. In the market place, the woman worker has generally been paid lower wages than the man and retained in a subordinate position without upward mobility. In the domestic sphere, unpaid housework and unpaid reproductive and child-rearing labour have been instrumental in shaping the condition of women. The nuclear family is perceived as a unit of private property, in which the wife–mother is exploited by the male as well as by the larger organisation of capitalism. As a result of the specific economic conditions of women, in which they are exploited by virtue of their gender, some materialist feminists have established women as a class, thus accommodating the gender oppression of women within the class analysis. Nevertheless, the notion of women as a class can obscure differences between upper-, middle- and working-class women.

The overriding gender-neutral quality of the materialist analysis has produced what has been termed the 'unhappy marriage' between materialism and feminism. When notions of class and production do not account for patriarchal institutions, they seem irreconcilable with a feminist consciousness. As in most unhappy marriages, there are two sides to the contradiction: from the materialist perspective, the radical-feminist position displays a dominant class bias in its universalist and essentialist mystification of economic and historical factors; from the radical-feminist perspective, the materialist-feminist position obscures the oppression of gender, creating mythical bridges between men and women of the same class and mythical divides between women of different classes. The radical feminists contend that the materialists omit the dynamics of sexual oppression and the materialists contend that sexual oppression can only be understood within capitalist (or other economic) modes of production.

Nevertheless, materialist feminists have sought to save the marriage with several strategies. By treating women as a class, they can analyse women's underemployment, unemployment and wage inequities with revised notions of surplus value. Women are identified as a kind of surplus labour force necessary for the enforcement of general lower wages, strike-breaking tactics and other controls over labour which serve the cause of the owners, or profit-makers. By extending this analysis into the domestic sphere, women as a free labour force in housework and reproduction serve both the male worker and the owner. The wife–mother reproduces the labourer in two ways: by producing future labourers as babies and by preparing the labourer for each day's work. Her unpaid labour represents money in the pocket of the worker, grants him leisure-time privileges she does not herself enjoy, and provides the owners with labourers at no supply cost.

The influence of the materialist analysis has created new areas of internal clarification in the feminist movement. The notion of class consciousness has called attention to the predominance of upper-middle-class women in the feminist movement. The nature of this class bias accounts for certain elements in the ideology and cultural achievements of the movement and the relative inability of the movement to embrace poor women and women of colour. This new consciousness has created a dialogue of differences within the movement, leading to the identification of new socio-economic issues and new dynamics of consciousness-raising. The interaction between the discoveries of radical feminism and those of materialist feminism is lively and productive. Readers who wish to do further research in this area will find many authors who provide clear studies of the issues, including Sheila Rowbotham, Zillah Eisenstein, Heidi Hartmann and Nancy Hartsock.

The influence of materialist feminism on feminist theatre has been most pronounced in Britain and other European countries, while in the United States it has been minor. The examples cited in this chapter are therefore all drawn from Europe. Most of the plays and practices cited illustrate a happy marriage of materialism and feminism, though some also dramatise the problems in the relationship.

Class and sex

Two plays by Caryl Churchill demonstrate the way in which a materialist class analysis can work together with a feminist analysis of sexual–gender oppression to create dramatic action. *Cloud Nine* (1979) couples colonialism in the political and economic sense with colonialism of a sexual nature. This deadly duo go hand in hand through the territory of Africa, creating internal strife and destruction in the relationships among members of the family unit as well as in the relations between races. Cross-gender, cross-racial and cross-generational casting foregrounds the fabricated roles such colonialism creates, distancing identity from biology. In Act I, the native servant is played by a white man, the little boy is played by a mature woman and the mature woman is played by a man. The casting of these roles reproduces the hierarchical, oppressive structure of class and gender privilege: white men determine the roles native servants and women must play, and adults determine the actions of children. The wife–mother, Betty, is played by a man. Her opening lines state that she is everything that men want her to be. The cross-gender casting dramatises this patriarchal colonisation of female experience by allowing the audience to see the man behind the image. The image of the native servant, playing by a white man, works in the same way.

Act I also exposes the complicity of political and economic colonialism with the institution of compulsory heterosexuality. The politico-economic order enjoys a reciprocal relationship with the dominant sexual order: to infringe the one is to threaten the other. Covert homosexual relations abound, but the characters who participate in them are chastised for their disruption of both orders. A man and a woman who have already expressed homosexual attractions to others are compelled to marry, and their marriage is characterised as necessary for the maintenance of Britain's colonial supremacy. The dramatic objective of Act I is to show how the colonial system of privilege and oppression is maintained: beating natives instils fear; berating women leads them into self-accusation; repressing sexual freedom produces guilt.

In Act II, contemporary Londoners explore new economic and sexual choices. Relative economic and sexual independence produces a variety of human relationships rather than the single option of heterosexual monogamy. In the materialist manner, the success of these relationships is determined as much by economics and history as by personal preference. Proximity to colonial history makes the habit of sexual ownership threaten the freedom of experimentation. A feminist framework surrounds the arena of sexuality. Though the play is about both male and female relationships, the boundaries of its dramatic structure are set by the female character of the wife–mother. The situation of this woman both sets up and resolves the dramatic action. In Act I she images the assimilation of women's identities by patriarchal roles. Near the end of Act II, she has a monologue of liberation in which she recovers her own body, her own sexual desire and her own financial independence.

Top Girls (1982) combines a focus on women with a focus on the conditions of production. Since the play has no parts for male characters, it concentrates exclusively on the experiences of women. Act II, which concerns the relationship between women's gender roles and the market place, opens in an office – a site of labour and production. The leading character, Marlene, is an upwardly mobile boss, a successful businesswoman who exhibits the privileges of her position in her power over the other women in the office. Her upward mobility has made her male-identified distancing her from the other women around her. Yet the real drama of class and feminist consciousness occurs between Marlene and her sister (a familiar feminist metaphor). Marlene returns to her home town to visit her sister, who is confined to the labour of unpaid housework and child-rearing. The class difference between the sisters are dramatised in several kinds of interactions questions of personal style and politics, attitudes towards other members of the family, hopes for the future and regard for the past. Finally, it is revealed that the sister is using her financial resources and labour to raise Marlene's own child. This characterises Marlene's upward mobility as a colonisation of her own sister for her class achievement. she is using her sister as kind of surplus labour that increases her own opportunities for profit. The economic situation has created two choices for women: the relative economic poverty of child-rearing, or the emotional alienation of success within the structures of capitalism.

Dusa, Fish, Stas and Vi (1976), by Pam Gems, centres on the problematic intersection between Marxist political work and a feminist consciousness. The principal character is named Fish (the play was formerly titled *Dead Fish*), whose political situation is described in the cast list: 'having considered the inadvertency of her [class] privilege, and the mores of middle-class values, she has attached herself to a political group on the left'. In the middle of the play, Fish breaks through the 'fourth wall' to speak directly to the audience about the work of a real-life Marxist leader – Rosa Luxemburg. She uses the example of Luxemburg to describe the relationship between feminism and Marxism, posing the question, 'so why is Rosa Luxemburg relevant?' She answers by listing some of Luxemburg's historical achievements, and concludes,

> Rosa demonstrates that the emergence of women thinkers in politics modifies Marxist theory as we know it . . . to be outside [Marxism] may be oppression. To be inside may well be total irrelevancy. . . . The nature of the social and political contribution of women is, at the moment, wholly in question. Is feminism to be an increasing power elite in a given existing structure?

Fish then enumerates the many personal losses which Rosa suffered, noting that 'usually when people write about her nowadays they leave all that out. They are wrong.' She makes the point that the personal is also the political and that the traditional leftist practice of separating political work from romantic, personal and sexual fulfilment is incorrect.

However, the plot reveals that Fish finds herself participating in this same painful schism between political practice and personal life. Her leftist boyfriend deserts her for a woman who is 'dependent'. In spite of his Marxist ideology, he is beginning to act like a member of the bourgeoisie, 'walking about with pot plants under his arm!' Fish is obsessed with his new relationship; she cannot reconcile his political commitment with his personal behaviour. In spite of her perception that his personal desires are politically incorrect, she is unable to detach herself from her feelings for this man, nor comprehend the nature of their previous relationship, which had seemingly combined political work with personal commitment. In the end, Fish commits suicide. The play dramatises the 'unhappy marriage' as such.

Ironheart (*Eisenherz*, 1981), a German play by Gerlind Reinshagen, deals with the psychological and sexual effects that wage and promotional inequities have upon women. The entire play takes place in an office, focusing on women in clerical jobs – one of the main areas of employment for working women. However, Reinshagen carefully distinguishes her characters along class lines. The office head officiously demands punctuality, attention to details and strict obedience from her staff. She is an ex-countess, who manifests her class's exercise of power and its attendant isolation, decadence and depression. Then a young man comes to work in the office. In spite of his lack of experience, desultory working-habits and mediocre mental abilities, he possesses the potential for upward mobility, a potential the countess and the other women will never enjoy.

The women discuss other men who have 'passed through' their ranks, exhibiting the privileges of their power in various destructive ways, such as through affairs and abrupt desertions. As the men rise in the ranks of power, their desires demand women who match their new class status. These secretaries are left behind, scarred by their abandonment. Reinshagen draws several intriguing character developments from this privileged sexual behaviour. One woman has begun to seek out masochistic relationships, sporting her bruises and cuts like medals of accomplishment to make her the centre of attention in the office – a painful bid for social power. The women also discuss the way in which the male's presence changes their discourse: their elliptical style, dependent upon mutual understanding, becomes impossible confronted by his distant, rational discourse. Though this issue is reminiscent of the radical feminists' focus on women's language, Reinshagen presents it in the context of class and the economic ladder of power, rather than in that of a gender attribute.

The play takes its title from the nickname ('Ironheart') given to the youngest woman on the staff. She is the positive character, who observes the troubled existence of her co-workers and ultimately leaves the office in search of a more promising career. Her decision to leave is prompted by the suicide of a young woman in the neighbouring office; 'Ironheart' witnesses her leap from the window and immediately packs up her own belongings. In fact, the neighbouring office has been visible during the entire play, with a cast of characters just like the central ones. This device underlines the fact that the play is not about unique individuals, but rather dramatises a specific socio-economic situation that prevails throughout the system. The experiences of the characters are determined by the prevailing mode of production within patriarchal capitalism. The primary dramatic action of the characters is to work. The conclusion of the play suggests that the work in the office will continue as it always has, and that any painful consequences produced by this mode of production cannot disrupt the order of the system.

Gerlind Reinshagen is the most established woman playwright in West Germany. The majority of her plays have been produced in the major state theatres and directed by the leading contemporary directors. Her plays represent the experiences and attitudes of the generation of German women who grew up during the Nazi period. Friederike Roth is a younger playwright whose plays dramatise the lives of women who have grown up in post-war Germany. The title of her most celebrated play, *Ritt auf die Wartburg* (1981), suggests a journey up the hill where the Wartburg castle is located. In the play a small group of West German women decide to take their vacation in East Germany. The contradictions they discover between capitalist West Germany and communist East Germany are central to the comedy of the play. Yet these political differences are revealed in settings appropriate to women, such as a hair salon and a dance hall (where they meet East German men). The feminist issues of aging as sex objects and sexual relationships with men are defined within the contrasting economic and political structures of divided German society.

A French play, *The Singular Life of Albert Nobbs* (*La Vie singulière d'Albert Nobbs*, 1977), by Simone Benmussa, offers a materialist analysis of cross-dressing. Albert Nobbs is a nineteenth-century woman who has lived her life as a man in order to obtain a better wage. She can 'pass' as a man and works as a waiter in a hotel, occupying a position with more power and better money than enjoyed by a maid. Albert meets another woman who has lived her life as a man. She tells Albert that she has found happiness by marrying a woman, with whom she shares a home, domestic labour and friendly support. Albert begins to fantasise about such a marriage and sharing her home with a woman. Though she longs for the companionship this marriage would provide, she has no interest in sex or romantic love, being primarily interested in the economic and domestic gain such a union might provide. Albert begins to court one of the maids, who is interested in Albert's money and the favours it can buy her. When Albert proves to be financially conservative and sexually backward (she does not reveal her true gender to the maid), the maid deserts her. Albert spends the rest of her life alone, hoarding her money and hiding it in small packets around her room. Near the end of the play she dies, frozen in the act of polishing shoes.

Though gender is constantly foregrounded by Albert's drag role and by her courtship of another woman, the materialist perspective retains a focus on the economics of the situation. Class issues are compounded with the privileges of the male gender in the relationships between Albert and the 'female' maids. Gender appears as a socio-economic role that determines the access one has to money. 'Drag' is an economic necessity for women who desire upward mobility, but the fiction of their gender prevents them from obtaining satisfaction in their personal lives. Most of the scenes take place in the hotel. Albert's inner life develops while she works, placing the internal dynamics of character within the conditions of labour.

Italian materialist feminism may be represented by a series of one-woman plays entitled *Female Parts*, written by Franca Rame and her husband, Dario Fo.[1] The comedy in several of these monologues relies upon the frantic pace of a woman overloaded with the double duties of a job and domestic labour. *Waking Up* is a monologue by a woman with a factory job, a baby and a sleeping husband. While getting her baby ready to go to child care before she catches the bus to work, she frantically searches for her keys. The search leads her to reconstruct the activities of the prior evening. In so doing, she recounts an argument with her husband that raises the familiar leftist issues about the exploitation of workers, but with a feminist slant: 'Listen Luigi, I said, You get mad about how nobody pays you for your travelling time but what about me? Do I get paid for all the working and slaving I do at home? No I do not. And believe you me everything I do here is for the multinational, oh yes!' She articulates the issue of unpaid housework, adding that of the reproduction of the male worker: 'We recondition you, regenerate you . . . reproduce you! And all for free!' Meanwhile, the woman continues to wash the baby and search for her keys, while her husband continues sleeping. After telling how she berated him for exploiting her, she ironically describes his male Marxist response: 'he had a real Self-Criticism session and he was so good at it it made me cry'. Apparently the self-criticism did not change his leisure habits, since he continues to sleep while she works. The play problematises the personal–political relationship between married Marxists, underlining the exploitation of the wife in the domestic sphere. This situation creates marital problems when the wife has a Marxist-feminist perspective and the husband does not. Basically, however, the Marxist-feminist critique notes that marital problems are caused by the corporation that profits from the unpaid labour of both husband and wife.

In the monologue *The Same Old Story*, Rame stages the exploitation of women within the context of sexual responsibility and abortion. The woman mimes intercourse, stopping periodically to remind the man that she is not using a birth-control device. He continues, driving towards his own orgasm at her expense. Once again, her partner is a male leftist to whom she says, 'and you're supposed to be the big militant radical. . . . Do you know what you are? A big radical prick. Yes and that's who your real comrade is . . . your prick! That's the one who's a reactionary imperialist ecclesiastical capitalist royalist . . . puppet!' Exploited by her sexual partner, she becomes pregnant only to discover that she will also be exploited by the male doctors who are licensed to give abortions. She deduces that the doctors who are pro-life take that stance to prevent public clinics from giving cheap abortions, enabling them to charge large amounts for doing the job privately.

Rame dramatises male sexual irresponsibility as an exploitation of women that parallels the capitalist exploitation of workers. The humour relies on the male leftist's inability to perceive the connection between a sexual, personal exploitation and the economic variety. The woman becomes the revolutionary subject in the domestic domain as the worker is in the international one.

The male leftist is unaware that he reproduces the conditions of exploitation and domination in the domestic scene, acting like an owner, in bed and in the home. It is this unconscious collusion with dominant economic practices, rather than gender alone, that is the cause of his behaviour. There is no notion of patriarchy as such in Rame's Marxist-feminist texts: instead, the privileges accorded to the male gender are seen as an extension of capitalist production modes and class privilege into the personal, domestic sphere. Women appear as an exploited class within an exploited class. The vocabulary of Marxist thought is used to describe their condition and hurled as insults at the leftist men. Though the plays dramatise a lack of understanding on the part of male Marxists, they are not intended as final critiques. Rather, they are located in the tradition of socialist realism, aimed at educating the men and women in the audience.

Work on materialist feminist theatre groups, as opposed to individual playwrights, has been concentrated in Britain, which is where the best-documented studies of the subject have been published. Michelene Wandor, in her book *Understudies: Theatre and Sexual Politics*, describes the development of most of the internationally known British troupes and their relationship to political thought and action. Catherine Itzin, in her book *Stages in the Revolution: Political Theatre in Britain since 1968*, devotes several chapters to the rise of feminist thought in leftist troupes. Since these two authors have covered this area so completely, this book will not include a discussion of materialist feminist groups. However, the theatre practice of materialist feminists will be represented by a brief description of explorations towards an acting style combining elements from both Marxist and feminist theatre.

In an interview, Gillian Hanna, co-founder of the Monstrous Regiment, explores the possible connection between the staging of feminist plays and the Brechtian acting tradition. Hanna begins with the political point that there is 'an urgent necessity to find the dialectical relationship between socialism and feminism – to demonstrate that the two are inseparable – i.e. there will not be a socialist revolution without feminism and that a feminist revolution will not be achieved without socialism.'[2] Hanna's materialistic feminist position shifts the emphasis from production in the classic Marxist sense, located in the factory, to the 'material change which occurs between men and women at a point of conflict'. Hanna believes that the way to portray this political moment on the stage is to combine the acting techniques of Stanislavski's Method with those of Brecht's Epic style. The Method can be used to portray the internal, emotional and psychological dynamics of the personal conflict between men and women, while Brecht's Epic acting-style can be used to portray the social significance of that internal state. Specifically, for Hanna, the Brechtian technique would demonstrate the social significance of male–female relationships to the audience. This combination of acting techniques would reflect the feminist combination of personal and political.

How does this project compare with the radical feminist acting style explored by Wittig and Zeig? Whereas the objective of the Zeig–Wittig project is to break down notions of gender related to the representation of the 'female' body on stage, the aim of Hanna's project is to represent material change in male–female relationships. Like the materialist-feminist plays discussed above, Hanna's style places the dramatic emphasis on the relationship between men and women and the necessity for change. By contrast, radical feminist plays and acting styles are directed exclusively at women and their interrelationships. Consequently, while materialist-feminist productions rarely depict a lesbian relationship, radical feminist ones give little attention to heterosexual relationships. Moreover, materialist feminist theatre practice is aimed at a mixed audience of men and women. Hanna notes that the Monstrous Regiment is looking for a new audience by 'playing in clubs, community halls, town halls'. The radical feminist troupes seek out female audiences, playing in women's prisons, for women's political rallies, or including all-women nights in the runs of each play.

Though there are crucial differences between the radical feminist and the materialist feminist positions, both have created a viable tradition of playwriting and theatre production. The interaction between these two positions has enriched the feminist movement and feminist theatre practice by creating a dialogue of differences and by extending the feminist critique. The influence of their ideas and practices has begun to foster the sense of an international feminist theatre tradition, including authors and troupes in Europe and North America. These two positions have been seminal in the creation and development of feminist theatre. Yet, in the latter part of the 1970s, a new position emerged that radically altered feminist thought and practice, a position that caused a revision of the feminist perspective on the movement's own internal development – the position of women of colour.

Chapter 6

Women of Colour and Theatre

Because this description of the position and project of women of colour has been written by a white author, the discourse is necessarily distanced from the actual experiences which shape this position. The distance is not an objective distance, but one which reflects a perspective of racial and class privilege. The white author cannot write from the experience of racial oppression, or from the perspective of the ethnic community, and must thus omit a sense of the internal composition of such a community or of its interface with the dominant white culture. Moreover, within the study of feminism and theatre, this distance creates crucial problems in research and criticism. Many of the materials on ethnic feminist theatre practice and writing are difficult to obtain, which reflects the alternative nature of the project. The companies concerned are relatively poor and often short-lived, requiring the critic either to have access to their productions, press releases and reviews (often in small presses), or to interview artists in the field. The distance of the white author from the ethnic community creates a critical absence of such contacts and research opportunities. This distance has influenced all of the information in this chapter, but is most evident in the restriction of its focus to examples from the United States, drawn primarily from the work of black women and Chicanas.

Among the theatrical achievements of women of colour, those of black women have become the most accessible to critics working within the dominant white culture. The white critic can obtain reviews and critical articles in familiar publications. However, this method of research leads the critic to review works which have been produced primarily within traditional theatre – a perspective reflected in this chapter. Although there do not seem to be any records of black feminist theatre groups, this impression may simply reflect the situation of the white critic. The records and critical perspective on Chicanas in theatre are accessible because of the work of Yvonne Yarbro-Bejarano, which has been published in several available sources.[1] Other minority women have their own histories, traditions and experiences, which have affected the way they write for the theatre or practise the art – particularly women working in Asian-American theatre and as Native American story-tellers. It is to be hoped that future feminist critics and historians will pursue studies in these fields. Though this chapter is severely limited in its scope, no book on the intersection of feminism and theatre could hope to provide a relatively complete overview of the topic without some attempt to represent the position of women of colour. To this end, the reader is once more reminded that this material is designed merely to draw the broad parameters of these women's position and to offer a sampling of its application to texts and practices within two specific ethnic communities.

Separating the position of women of colour from other feminist positions ghettoises these women and their work as they have been ghettoised traditionally. Ideally, the work of these women would be grouped with that of others around 'colour-blind' issues. The same might be said about the treatment of lesbian women in Chapter 4. However, women of colour have identified their position as a discrete issue within feminism, challenging the presumed homogeneity of voice and vision within the movement. The term 'women of colour' entered common parlance in the last years of the 1970s, signifying both a weakness and a strength within the feminist movement. The weakness resides in the predominantly white composition of the movement and the relative insensitivity to issues of ethnic oppression that this entails. The strength resides in the creation of a coalition of all women of colour, who may previously have worked only in their respective ethnic communities.

The position of women of colour fuses aspects of both

materialist feminism and radical feminism. The materialist critique of class is central to women of colour, whose ethnic communities are often bound by both colour and class. The understanding of the hierarchical nature of classes under capitalism is essential to understanding the oppressive nature of racism. When ethnic identity is used to relegate people of colour to the role of surplus value in the labour force, race becomes identical with class in the market place. Furthermore, the association of certain ethnic communities with particular modes of production explains the way in which women of colour are ghettoised. Black women and Chicanas are concentrated in the lowest-paid sectors of the labour force – in the service occupations, textile and other manufacturing industries – which are also those most affected by economic shifts. Racial stereotypes serve to bolster the privileges of class – for example, in the association of black women and Chicanas with the occupations of house-keeper, maid and farm-worker. A class analysis of women of colour aids the white feminist to perceive the difference between her situation and that of a woman of colour. The woman of colour bears the triple burden of gender, racial and class oppression, while the white woman benefits from her class privilege of colour.

The radical-feminist analysis aids in the comprehension of the sexual roles to which women of colour are confined within both the dominant white culture and within their own ethnic communities. Within the dominant culture, recent feminist analyses of pornography reveal the emphasis on bondage, violation and domination in the sexualised images of women of colour. Sexual aggression and violation are built into the desire the white male feels when viewing pornographic images of these women, duplicating the dynamics of colonisation that white culture has imposed upon ethnic peoples. Within their own ethnic communities, women of colour are often regarded as the sexual property of their men. This can imply their confinement to the home and domestic labour, or it can explain their relegation to a role of support: the male takes the role of leader, spokesperson, artist or even political organiser, while the female is expected to play the role of follower, listener and general aide.[2]

Women of colour have described the feminist movement as primarily an upper-middle-class white women's movement. They point out that, although the movement has produced numerous publications, productions and networks designed to overcome the dominant gender bias, it often replicates the racist and classist one. For example, in 1981 the American Theater Association held its first national pre-conference for women. The pre-conference was entitled 'The New Girl Network'. During its sessions, several black women called attention to the fact that this new network duplicated the all-white standards of the patriarchal order. In *Theater News*, Elizabeth Hadley Freydberg characterised the programme in her article 'Black Women and Feminism: One More Time (How Many More Times?)': 'I told the group exactly how they appeared to me; that I thought the network was already established and completed before anyone arrived. . . . I didn't expect that this group would make the same mistake of excluding blacks and other traditionally ignored groups, but it seemed that they were.'[3]

Women of colour have also pointed out that most consciousness-raising groups have been composed primarily of white women and that they have rarely dealt with issues of racism and class bias. Thus, the perspective on issues identified by CR groups as feminist issues reflects only white women's experiences. For example, the issue of reclaiming the body from sexual colonisation (see Chapter 4) does not account for the differences between the sexual colonisation of women of colour and that of white women. In the arts, images of white women's bodies abound, while images of women of colour are infrequent. Famous paintings of nudes and the sexualised roles of women in the 'masterpieces' of the theatre rarely feature the image or character of a woman of colour. Whereas art misrepresents the bodies of white women, it generally ignores those of women of colour. On the other hand, when the sexuality of women of colour is represented, it often betrays a class bias. The woman of colour is generally not represented as the elegant, upper-class model, a potential marriage-partner, rather, she represents the object of illicit sexual desire. Moreover, to the extent that white women in CR groups have concentrated on their own experiences, developing the notion of 'sisters' or of the commonality of women's experiences, they have avoided articulating the differences between themselves and women of colour or addressing issues important to working-class women, such as under- and unemployment or forced sterilisation. In fact, they have avoided the critique these women have created about the role of white women, and have not dealt with the anger women of colour feel about the class privileges of white feminists.

Audre Lorde, in her article 'The Uses of Anger: Women Responding to Racism', describes the necessary interchange between white feminists and women of colour as well as the positive role the expression of anger can play in such a situation:

> Any discussion among women about racism must include the recognition and use of anger. This discussion must be direct and creative because it is crucial. We cannot let our fear of anger deflect us nor seduce us into settling for anything less than the hard work of excavating honesty. . . . Anger is a grief of distortions between peers, and its object is change . . . for black women and white women to face each other's angers without denial or immobility or silence or guilt is in itself a heretical and generative idea. It implies peers meeting upon a common basis to examine difference, and to alter those distortions which history has created around our difference. . . . CR groups in the past, largely white, dealt with how to express anger, usually at the world of men . . . there was usually little attempt to articulate the genuine differences between women, such as those of race, color, age, class, and sexual identity.[4]

This anger felt against white women was dramatised in a monologue performed by the black actress Beah Richards at the first National Women's Theatre Festival in Santa Cruz:

> And you,
> women,
> seeing, spoke no protest.
> But cuddled down in your pink slavery
> and thought somehow my wasted blood
> confirmed your superiority.[5]

The feminist movement has acknowledged its racist bias and made anti-racism one of its central tenets. As far back as the first issue of *Ms.* magazine (a well-known feminist magazine in the United States), opposition to racism was listed as a basic tenet of feminism. In the late 1970s, many white feminists began participating in workshops and CR groups around racism, and a number of feminist critics have begun to include works by women of colour in every discussion of women's literature and art. Yet, in spite of the seeming centrality of the issue of racism within the movement, the majority of feminist plays by white women continue to dramatise only the lives of white women; many feminist theatre productions have not practised colour-blind or interracial casting, and feminist theatre groups have not created interracial audiences. On the other hand, several women of colour have risen to prominence in the theatre, creating new plays for women in their own ethnic communities, practising acting-techniques which reflect their ethnic backgrounds, and developing from among their own communities audiences for their productions.

Black women and the theatre

In the United States, black women have been the pioneers and foremost spokeswomen in the movement of women of colour. The movement for black independence in the 1960s had already provided them with an ethnic consciousness, a familiarity with political organisation and a language of protest that could be combined with a feminist critique. In fact, these achievements of the black liberation movement aided the feminist movement at large in its articulation of oppression. Likewise, for several decades now, black women playwrights have been achieving commercial and critical success in the theatre. In 1956, Alice Childress's play *Trouble in Mind* won the Obie award for the best off-Broadway play of the season. In 1959, Lorraine Hansberry's *A Raisin in the Sun* won the New York Drama Critics Circle award for the best play of the year. In 1964, Adrienne Kennedy's *Funnyhouse of a Negro* won an Obie Distinguished Play award. In 1970, Ntozake Shange's *for colored girls who have considered suicide when the rainbow is enuf* was an outstanding commercial success on Broadway, as was Vinnette Carroll's *Don't Bother Me, I Can't Cope* in 1972. Among other successful black women playwrights, mention should be made of Sonia Sanchez, J. E. Franklin, Elaine Jackson and Martie Charles. Most of the plays of these women focus on the experiences of

black women and several of them illuminate the position of the
black women in the theatre.

In two plays, *Florence* (1949) and *Trouble in Mind*, Alice
Childress dramatises the oppression the black actor endures
within her profession. Florence never appears in the play of that
name, but her mother relates what professional opportunities
were available to her: a Broadway play in which she was cast as a
maid and a film made for black audiences. In other words, the
actor Florence is relegated to the same role in theatre production
as her black counterpart plays in the society at large – the role of
the maid. Additionally, her role in the theatre reflects the same
class bias as that suffered by the maid: the role is a marginal one,
ensuring relative invisibility and bringing paltry financial reward.
Florence's other option for work is to be ghettoised, separated
from the dominant culture – she can find some work in all-black
productions. During the play, Florence is characterised as
unemployed and desperately in need of money, a situation
created by the scarcity of texts with black roles and the casting-
practice which interprets most lead roles as white ones. *Trouble
in Mind* presents the encounter between a black actor and the
racist assumptions of her director. In the original version of the
play, the actor eventually rallies the cast to her cause and leads a
walk-out. The play suggests that a black political consciousness
and protest can be applied to the institution of the theatre. The
play also depicts the positive role the expression of anger can play
among peers, as the actor successfully gains support from the
other members of her cast.

In Adrienne Kennedy's *A Movie Star Has to Star in Black and
White* (1976), the central character is a black playwright, Clara.
Clara's creative imagination merges characters and scenes from
her own life with scenes from Hollywood movies. The characters
in her own life are black and the movie stars are white – thus the
pun in the title. The black-and-white play splices scenes with
glamorous movie stars, such as Bette Davis and Paul Henreid or
Montgomery Clift and Shelley Winters, with scenes with poor
black characters. At times, the movie stars speak in the familiar
dialogue of their movies; at others, they tell the story of Clara.
The high melodrama of the Hollywood movies conveys the strong
emotions Clara feels about the members of her family, but this
coupling also ironises the cultural assimilation of such feelings by

an all-white industry of the imagination such as Hollywood movies. The play demonstrates how the absence of black actors and black stories in the culture affects the ability of the black playwright to generate new narratives about her life. Kennedy has extended this experience into the confrontation between a black playwright and the history of the canon in *The Owl Answers* (1969). The black playwright travels to London, excited to see the historical monuments of her craft. Instead, she discovers that this past did not 'parent' her, as historical characters are contradicted by images of her own black parents. Both plays show the internal conflict of the black playwright who has absorbed the white symbols and characters of the dominant culture only to discover the contradictions between that realm and the realm of her personal experience. In Kennedy's plays, the realm of racist oppression is an internal one, but the issues of marginality, invisibility and assimilation are the same. Though Kennedy's plays are not explicitly feminist, her leading female characters situate the effects of racism within a female subject.

Kennedy's plays dramatise the relationship between the black woman in theatre and the white canon. Because the institution of theatre rarely practises colour-blind or interracial casting, the black actor has little hope of performing in the classic roles for women. Nevertheless, some black actors have successfully played in Shakespearean roles. As early as the nineteenth century, Henrietta Vinton Davis toured a one-woman show of Shakespearean pieces. Though her show was a critical and commercial success, Davis always appeared alone and never became part of a Shakespearean company. In the twentieth century, several directors and companies have cast interracial Shakespearian productions: Jane White, Ruby Dee and Beah Richards have all created famous Shakespearean roles. The book *Shakespeare in Sable* by Erroll Hill traces the history of this practice.

Though this is a positive practice, it also generally means that the black actor must shed all traces of black culture in order to play the famous roles: she must learn to walk, talk and look like women in the white culture. At the first National Women's Theatre Festival (Santa Cruz, California, 1983), Beah Richards, an actor who has appeared in several Shakespearean productions, performed the audition piece she had never been allowed to use –

a Shakespearean soliloquy in the rhythms and intonations of a black dialect, with its attendant gestures and blocking. Richards played all of the dramatic beats inherent in the soliloquy, but within her own ethnic cultural style, drawing attention to the way the canon suppresses a black woman's voice, body language and, concomitantly, her style of fashion, make-up, bone structure and hair style. The audience was also led to consider the effects on the black actor of stage-lighting, costuming and blocking designed for white actors. One of the pieces in *Narratives: A Dramatic Event*, a collective collage of monologues, concerns the need for a black actor to have her hair straightened for her portfolio pictures:

> the straightening iron; sado-masochistic artifact
> salvaged from some chamber of the Inquisition
> and given new purpose in the new world.
> What was there
> about straight hair
> that made me want to suffer . . . to have it?
> made me a recluse
> on any rainy, snowy, hot, or humid day,
> away from any activity that produced the least
> moisture to the scalp
> most of all sex . . .
> my beautician gave me a pick
> and told me no cock was worth so drastic a change.
> I struggled to be liberated from the supremacy
> of straight hair.[6]

Perhaps these factors in dominant theatre production have contributed to the rise of the one-woman show performed by the black actor. In this context she can design all the elements of production to fit her image and experience. These shows are generally composed of original material written by the actor as well as selections from other authors, including poetry, short stories and pieces of dialogue. This form also reflects, in its combination of acting and story-telling, the emphasis on the oral tradition in black culture. Tarzana Beverly, Beah Richards and Whoopi Goldberg are some of the women who have recently been successful in this genre. In 1984, Goldberg became the first black woman to take such a show to Broadway. Goldberg created six different characters, from a male drug-addict to a twelve-year-old Los Angeles Valley girl. Though black women have not concentrated on creating feminist theatre groups, they have adapted this genre to productions of feminist and ethnic materials. The centrality of the dramatic monologue in the productions of black actors has also influenced the texts of black playwrights: for example, Ntozake Shange's *for colored girls* is essentially a collage of monologues.

Though black women have distinguished themselves as playwrights and actors, only a few black women have been able to work as directors. In fact, all women encounter extreme difficulties in becoming a director because of the executive power associated with the role. The director is in charge of actors (often predominantly male) and designers (almost exclusively male). Often, a woman director must discover a way to exercise this power without disrupting traditional gender roles. Women directors report that behaviour considered capable in males is considered aggressive and offensive in females. Some assume a motherly role in the execution of their duties.[7] For women of colour, the assumption of such executive powers defies gender roles, racial and class stereotypes. In spite of this handicap, a few black women have succeeded in this profession. Vinnette Carroll is a professional director who won the Drama Critics Circle award for distinguished directing in 1972, and Ellen Stewart has distinguished herself as a director and as the founder of her own theatre, La Mama. Stewart migrated to New York because she heard that 'coloured' people could go to design school there, but instead of attending design school she began her own theatre in 1961. Beginning in a basement, Stewart's company struggled to survive in New York without critical attention or funds. In 1965, when she discovered she could receive more critical attention in Europe, Stewart opened La Mama in Paris. The company began its rise to fame, performing new plays by playwrights who would later become part of theatre history, such as Jean-Claude Van Itallie. Today, Stewart's theatre is one of the most influential counter-theatre groups in the United States. Yet Stewart is not known as a black director, nor is her theatre associated with black plays, or black feminist plays. Stewart is one of the few black women directors and founders of a theatre in the United

States to have achieved a national reputation and followed a 'colour blind' career.

For readers wishing to pursue further research in this area, there are materials available on black women playwrights. Additionally, there are a number of books on the history of black theatre in the United States. Outside a few feminist studies of black women playwrights, there is little published information on feminism and black women in theatre. Many black women work in the theatre on black issues, but only a few approach them from the perspective of feminism. Recent books such as Bell Hook's *From Margin to Center* outline the black woman's position on feminism, contrasting it to the white woman's. Hook's chapter on the relationship between women of colour and the men in their communities may explain the concentration of black women in ethnic theatre and the absence of a black feminist theatre movement.

Chicanas

'Chicana' is the feminine form of the generic term 'Chicano'. The Chicano may be defined as a person of Mexican ancestry living in the United States. 'Chicano' is a term of ideological and political self-definition, adopted by the Chicano movement in the mid 1960s. It is not generally accepted by all people in the country with Mexican ancestry, who may choose to call themselves Mexicans or Mexican-Americans, but the political movement rejected the latter term as representing assimilation into the dominant culture. Chicano was originally a derogatory term applied to newly arrived undocumented Mexican migrant workers in the United States, with negative and working-class connotations among Mexican-Americans. The movement appropriated the term to signal a commitment to militant politics. Thus, the term 'Chicana' implies a woman of Mexican ancestry in the United States who has identified herself with a political movement dedicated to the liberation of her ethnic community.

Chicanas in theatre face the same problems as black women as regards stereotyped roles and the unwillingness of directors to adopt a colour-blind casting-policy. In contrast to the informal relationship between black women with ethnic and feminist politics and the established theatre, Chicanas have created an

organisation which serves to define their condition and their goals
in theatre work. In 1978, Women in Teatro was founded with the
following objectives: 'To stimulate all aspects of artistic growth,
to help identify problems that relate specifically to mujeres en
teatro [women in theatre], to establish a support group for
women in theater, and to maintain an open communication
network.'[8] This group meets quarterly in different cities in
California to identify contemporary issues for Chicanas in theatre
and to organise solutions for problems. In addition, it has placed
a representative on the board of the national organisation of
Chicano theatre groups, TENAZ (Teatros Nacionales de Aztlan),
to articulate the situation of women in Chicano theatre. By 1980,
the group identified these needs for Chicanas in theatre: 'the
need for women playwrights, producers and directors; the need
for strong women's roles and the needs of individual women,
such as child care'.[9]

In 1980 the San Jose chapter of Women in Teatro founded a
production arm of their organisation called Valentina Productions.
This group was dedicated to performing works by women and
about women. In 1981 they performed *Voz de la mujer* (*Voice of
the woman*), a collage of poetry, songs and monologues. The
production was bilingual, in Spanish and English, reflecting the
bilingual heritage of the Chicano community. Language is a
central issue for the Chicana, for much of the oppression of the
dominant culture is conveyed through the suppression of the
Spanish language. Even though many Western and South-western
states have large Chicano populations and rely upon Chicano
labour for their agriculture, legal documents, educational tools
and public notices are not consistently printed in both languages,
denying Chicano people access to important information about
the dominant social and legal codes. Yet the relationship of the
Chicana to language is more complicated than that. She may not
speak simply in one language or the other, but use rather her
community's own special language, a mixture of Spanish and
English. This separates her from both mainstream language
communities, making her a linguistic outsider in social discourse.
Thus, the bilingual *Voz de la mujer* resounded with the grass-
roots language of its ethnic community and with the oppression
dominant discourse creates.

The play offered a historical range of women's problems, from
the image of Sor Juana (see Chapter 2), through the revolutionary

period in Mexico, to the present-day Chicana. While a poem by Sor Juana was being performed, an actor portrayed her writing it. This stage picture was provocative in itself, since the patriarchal institution of the Catholic Church forbade Sor Juana to continue reading and writing – an issue she regarded as prejudicial to women. Here she was allowed her creative voice and it spoke to the community. This piece was followed by songs about women in the Mexican Revolution, with stage pictures of women bearing arms. Then came a variety of poems about the experiences of common women's lives, such as male–female relationships, housework and family problems. The final poem was 'La Chicana' by Phyllis Lopez, with the Chicana portrayed by the entire cast. The poem sees her as a woman who may represent a mixture of races, but whose colour and class keep her working in menial jobs.

Chicanas in theatre have created a form of their own called 'teatropoesia' that reflects their ethnic and historical position. The form is a fusion of poetry and theatre, in which 'the verbal, private world of the printed text is translated into action in time and space . . . the silent dialogue between the lone reader and the poem has been replaced by communication that is collective, social and public in nature'.[10] This form echoes the Chicano community's interest in the performance of poetry, either in readings or, more commonly, in song. Here, the community practice becomes a theatrical reality, adapted to feminist ends. Teatropoesia originated in 1974 with a piece entitled *Chicana*, created by Dorinda Morena and a group in San Francisco called Las Cucarachas (The Cockroaches). *Voz de la mujer* followed in the same tradition, and *Tongues of Fire*, produced by a group of independent artists, is a more recent example of the genre.

Tongues of Fire (1981) presents the experiences and poems of Chicana writers. One poem, 'Maria la O', by Barbara Brinson-Pineda, recounts the journey of a woman who migrated from Mexico to work on the land in the United States. The woman's journey never ends, as she follows the harvest of the crops around the country:

> Texas cotton, Michigan cherry,
> California grape,
> to the city's concrete bed,
> to an open road.[11]

The poem conveys the rootless existence of the migrant worker, who is unable to identify with any specific location or community. Her life is the endless harvesting of crops, alienated from the land she works on and the food she helps to produce by the economic practice of piecework. She can attain no permanent position, regular salary, benefits or personal rewards in a system in which her colour condemns her to the role of surplus labour, maintaining a system of production that maximises profit by exploitation. Another poem in the play, 'Arriaga', describes the overriding repressive influence of the Catholic Church on a young woman. This poem concerns the repression of sexual and emotional expression in women who live within an ethnic community dominated by Catholicism. By contrast, 'In a Red-neck Bar down the Street', by Sandra Cisneros ('red-neck' is slang for a working-class reactionary male), describes a woman who refuses to act in the way sexual stereotypes of women dictate that she should behave. The woman enjoys breaking the stereotype in the bar by drinking an entire bottle of beer while holding it in her teeth:

> Boy that crazy
> act every time gets them
> bartender runs over
> says lady don't
> do that again.

Teatropoesia is similar to the one-woman show performed by black women. Both forms are collages of literary works by women of colour, focusing on the experiences created by their ethnic identity and reflecting the lack of viable scripts, but the Chicanas perform in a group rather than alone.

However, Chicanas and other Latinas in the United States, who experience the same social, cultural and economic discrimination, have also created one-woman shows. In 1982, Cora Hill de Castañón performed *No me callarán, no me callaré* (*They Will Not Silence Me, I Will Not Be Silent*), a dramatic re-creation of the life of Sor Juana based entirely on her own words.[12] Rose Cano, in her piece *Self-Portrait*, portrays various characters in the Latino home. Cano's text, in choosing the home as the arena of her play, reflects the emphasis on the family unit in her ethnic community – both its supportive and its repressive elements. Cano begins with the thirteen-year-old retarded daughter, who interacts with her sister in an alert, humorous manner. The scene suggests the dependence of the child on her older sister for company and positive reinforcement. The Mexican house-keeper, who was injured earlier in her life and has difficulty walking, talks with the older sister about her life, about the importance of the family and about the necessary role the sister plays in the home. The following scenes are presented by the older daughter, who has decided to leave the home and try living independently from the family – perhaps in a community of peers. She reacts to the threats, pleas, tears and abuse of her parents, who deny her permission to leave. They depict the contradiction between the family-centred life of the Latino family and the independent 'Anglo' mode of living. The daughter is caught between the personal lifestyles of two cultures, with the contradictions embedded in each. The play represents the struggle of the Latina to live an independent life.

Though Chicanas in theatre have created an organisation for their needs as well as their own form, they do not enjoy a stable of playwrights. Unlike black women, Chicanas have not won national prizes as playwrights or attained national prominence as directors. Chicanas work in an alternative theatre tradition which is aimed directly at their ethnic community, and they have not become involved in the mainstream theatrical tradition. Because their texts are predominantly bilingual, they are relatively inaccessible to a general audience or readership. Moreover, considering the restrictions imposed by the Catholic Church, by the Latino family structure and by the status of the migrant farm-worker, they may encounter more obstacles in the path of performance than black women. However, the composition of Spanish-speaking communities in the United States is changing and the future of the Chicana in theatre may be radically altered. The increasing presence of people from countries in Central and Latin America is creating a wider sense of community, introducing politics and practices quite different from those indigenous to the United States. This situation may infuse Chicana theatre with new production practices and goals.

Coalition theatre

'Coalition theatre' is a term used to designate a group of women working together to dramatise issues that affect all women of colour and that reflect their interaction with the feminist movement. Rather than directing its productions at a specific ethnic community, this kind of theatre aims at audiences of women, composed predominantly of feminists. Spiderwoman is the best known of the few groups in this category. Based in New York, it is composed of three Native American women, two whites and one Hispanic. Their plays are more explicitly about feminist issues than about women of colour, but, since the texts often include personal stories and are not performed using the acting-style, diction and gestures characteristic of the dominant white culture, they convey a sense of ethnic identity. The group was founded in 1975 by three Cuna-Rappahannock Native American women. Muriel Miguel, the artistic director, traces her work in theatre to her grade-school performing troupe, the Little Eagles, who performed Native American dances. The trio continued working in their teens, calling themselves Thunderbirds. The name 'Spiderwoman' is taken from the Hopi goddess of creation. Spiderwoman was the originator of design and taught the Hopi people how to weave. Every design she created contained her spirit, so into each she wove a flaw through which her spirit could escape and be free.[13] The group defines its task as weaving the stories of women, based on the practice of story-telling which is central to Native American culture. The 'flaw' in its designs seems to be the ribald humour in the texts, derived from flaws in the characters of the actors themselves. Spiderwoman has performed several plays both at home and abroad. It is one of the few internationally known feminist theatres in the United States. The group members take a personal, experiential approach to texts, using the strengths and weaknesses of their own personalities to enhance their stories. For example, in *The Lysistrata Numbah* (1977) they adapted the classic Greek text to their own experiences by imitating the characters in the text, who gave up sex for peace. The actors had no sex during their rehearsal period, in order to personalise the experience. In 1975 the group created *Woman in Violence*, performing a slapstick portrayal of violence against women, including street violence, domestic battering and persona intimidation. The influence of radical feminism on this group is apparent in its texts, but its performances add the critique of colour.

Gathering Ground (1984), a collage of poetry, short stories and monologues taken from a book of the same name,[14] was produced for the stage by a collective of women of colour in Seattle. The pieces were written and performed by Asian-Americans, Native Americans, Chicanas and black women. Many of the pieces dramatise the interface between a particular ethnic culture and the dominant white society. In the Asian-American texts, the interface is provided by the dress, demeanour, manners and inner monologue suited to Asian women but rejected by mainstream society. The situations created in the black and Chicana pieces represent a similar source of conflict. One text, 'The White Horse Cafe', illustrates the kind of support that could be available in a coalition of colour. A Native American hitch-hiker is picked up by a racially mixed group of women on an outing. The white women in the car elect to stop at a nearby restaurant to eat. They are oblivious to the agitation this decision causes in the black woman in the group, who fears entering all-white restaurants, dreading the stares and possible aggression of the people eating there. Only the Native American is sensitive to her withdrawal, perceiving why she is hesitant to enter. From their shared situation, they find mutual support, entering together as a couple, rather than as isolated individuals. They are stronger because they have one another. Their coalition comes from a common experience of racial oppression which the white women never perceive and cannot comprehend in subtle social situations. *Gathering Ground* represents the hope in the position of women of colour. These women can find mutual support in their struggle, making their position visible and discovering the liberating aspects in the combination of ethnic politics and feminism.

Chapter 7

Towards a New Poetics

The New Poetics

During the 1980s, feminist theory has risen to prominence both within the feminist movement and within the context of dominant theoretical practices. Many academic disciplines, such as sociology, anthropology and political science, as well as those concerned with art and literature, have begun to alter their theoretical and methodological approaches to accommodate the strategies of feminist theory. Likewise, the new theories of post-structuralism, Lacanian psychoanalysis, semiotics and reception theory have been radically altered by the feminist discoveries in these fields. By 1985, feminist theory had taken its place in the mainstream of the philosophical and critical applications of ideas. Within the feminist movement, theory occupies a more problematic position. Many feminists consider the pursuit of theory to be elitist. They perceive its specialised discourse as a linguistic class bias that is inaccessible to working-class women, women of colour and the broad spectrum of women who have not enjoyed the privilege of higher education. Moreover, theory is characterised as separate from practice, luring feminists away from working on the issues of socio-political oppression and isolating them in the male-dominated realm of abstract ideas, commonly known as the 'ivory tower'. For this reason, it is useful to locate the project of feminist theory within the realm of political practice.

From within the theoretical project, it is crucial to remember that feminism began in the streets, with demonstrations against the oppression of women.[1] The commitment to change was taken up by women in all professions, including academics and critics. Women working in the field of education discovered not only that their professional positions were influenced by patriarchal prejudice, but also that their subject matter represented the sexist biases of the dominant culture. In preparing students to enter the market place, they realised they must change not only what they were thinking about, but also how they were thinking. Academics transformed the social issues of the movement into themes and methods for research and criticism. In theatre, feminists applied the social critique of the movement to both the organisation of theatre practice and the analytical perception of the art, mixing critical discoveries such as the sexualisation of women on stage, the omission of women's narratives, the paucity of strong roles for women and the invisibility of lesbians and women of colour on stage, with the economic issues of wage inequities, patriarchal hiring-practices and union representation. Feminist critics and historians began to reconstruct the history of women in theatre, using the goals of consciousness-raising groups and social activists: to make women visible, to find their voice, to recover the works that the dominant history suppressed and to explain the historical process of the suppression of women and its effect on their achievements. At the same time, critics used these political strategies to create new ways to read a play, to view a production and to deconstruct the canon of dramatic criticism.

Because raising the consciousness of women was from the start central to the social movement, and this in turn made it important to understand modes of perception, psychological factors and patterns of thought, a natural working alliance between artists, theorists, historians, critics and social activists was created. Artists created new roles for women to play in the laboratory of theatre, where the stage offered opportunities for women's narratives and dialogues largely denied in the history of the dominant culture. Feminist plays could stage a kind of utopian CR group, in which women could interact with a freedom of experience and expression not easily attained in their daily lives. Critics could aid in consciousness-raising by accurately identifying the psychological, cultural and educational controls on women's consciousness and suggesting alternative modes of perception. By the 1980s, the joint efforts of feminist activists, artists and intellectuals had created a basic vocabulary for feminism and a topography of its enterprise. The period of initial explorations was over.

Once the broad parameters of the feminist project had been discovered, the need for a more solid, theoretical base began to be perceived. The perception of the sexualisation of women's identities prompted investigations into the dominant psychological theories of sexual development. Feminist studies of Freudian theory illuminated the way in which sexist biases informed the practice of psychoanalysis as well as the general practice of therapy, which is derived from several Freudian assumptions. In France, Jacques Lacan created a revision of Freud, which adapted his theories to more contemporary discoveries. Soon feminists began publishing critiques of Lacan. At the same time, feminist cultural theorists began to deconstruct the dominant cultural codes that enforced the sexualisation of women in systems of representation, utilising the new discoveries in semiotics and reception theory to deconstruct the alliance between sign systems and the patriarchal order. In the arts, practitioners expressed a desire for an overview of their disparate works as well as a theoretical model for the alliance between aesthetics and the basic feminist analysis. For example, at the first National Women's Theatre Festival, in Santa Cruz in 1983, three of the oldest feminist theatres in the United States admitted that their broader analysis of women's oppressions had given way to plays about specific issues. In dwelling on specific problems, they felt that perhaps they were beginning to lose their sense of the basic overall feminist critique. All of these new critical projects began to embrace deeper, more theoretical issues as it was realised that the perception of images rests upon epistemology, the practice of dialogue rests upon the nature of discourse, and the forms of representation are determined by the dominant philosophical systems in the culture at large.

For theatre, the basic theoretical project for feminism could be termed a 'new poetics', borrowing the notion from Aristotle's *Poetics*. New feminist theory would abandon the traditional patriarchal values embedded in prior notions of form, practice and audience response in order to construct new critical models and methodologies for the drama that would accommodate the presence of women in the art, support their liberation from the cultural fictions of the female gender and deconstruct the valorisation of the male gender. In pursuit of these objectives, feminist dramatic theory would borrow freely: new discoveries about gender and culture from the disciplines of anthropology, sociology and political science; feminist strategies for reading texts from the new work in English studies; psychosemiotic analyses of performance and representation from recent film theory; new theories of the 'subject' from psychosemiotics, post-modern criticism and post-structuralism; and certain strategies from the project called 'deconstruction'. This 'new poetics' would deconstruct the traditional systems of representation and perception of women and posit women in the position of the subject.

For the reader who is unfamiliar with these new theories, an effective starting-point for the intersection of new theory with performance and feminist poetics may be found in the field of semiotics. Keir Elam, in his book *The Semiotics of Theatre and Drama*, defines semiotics as 'a science dedicated to the study of the production of meaning in society . . . its objects are thus at once the different sign systems and codes at work in society and the actual messages and texts produced thereby'.[2] Semiotics, when applied to theatre, explores how theatre communicates, or how theatre produces a meaning. The basic operatives in the production of meaning are the signifier (or sign) and the signified. The signifier is the ensemble of elements in a theatrical production that compose its meaning – the text, the actor, the stage space, the lights, the blocking, and so on. The signified is the meaning or message which is derived from this signifier by the 'collective consciousness' of the audience. So, for example, semiotics seeks to describe the way in which the set becomes a sign: how it signifies place, time, social milieu and mood. Semiotics also identifies and explores those elements of the actor's performance that signify character and objective to the audience.

Since the signified is produced by the recipient of the signifier, semiotics identifies several texts within a performance situation. The written text is only one of these and is not necessarily the definitive one. There is the text printed in a book and read as literature, the text the director reads preparing for rehearsal, the rehearsal text the actor uses, and the production text the audience receives as it watches the play. Semiotics proposes that each of these texts is different and discrete, retaining an equal status with the other ones and representing appropriate material for a critical response. The constitution of a performance text, separate but equal to the written one, implies new dimensions in the co-production of the text. The importance of the author's intent gives way to the conditions of production and the composition of the audience in determining the meaning of the theatrical event. This implies that there is no aesthetic closure around the text, separating it from the conditions of its production. The performance text is constituted by the location of the theatre, the price of the ticket, the attitude of the ushers and the response of the audience as well as by the written dialogue and stage directions.

This semiotic constitution of the performance text is useful to a feminist poetics. Because the composition of the audience is an element in the co-production of the play's meaning, the gender of the audience members is crucial in determining what the feminist play might mean. The practice of performing before all-women audiences excludes men from the co-production of the play's meaning. Within a patriarchal culture, this exclusion may provide the only way certain elements of women's experience can be signified within the 'collective consciousness' of the audience. The insistence upon an all-woman audience, then, becomes an essential part of the composition of the theatrical event, rather than a social statement of separatism or reverse sexism. Likewise, ticket prices, child care, the time of the performance and the location of the theatre also co-produce the performance text, positing the accessibility of the production to working-class women, single mothers or women of colour as part of the meaning of the play. The gender, class and colour of the audience replace the aesthetic traditions of form or the isolated conditions of the author's intent within the interpretative strategies of dramatic theory, firmly allying poetics with feminist politics.

Perhaps even more important is the notion of the cultural encoding of the sign (or signifier), the semiotic discovery that provides a radical alteration of poetic strategies of performance. This notion positions a feminist analysis at the very foundation of communication – in the sign itself. Cultural encoding is the imprint of ideology upon the sign – the set of values, beliefs and ways of seeing that control the connotations of the sign in the culture at large. The norms of the culture assign meaning to the sign, prescribing its resonances with their biases. For a feminist, this means that the dominant notions of gender, class and race compose the meaning of the text of a play, the stage pictures of its production and the audience reception of its meaning. By describing the cultural encoding in a sign, semiotics reveals the covert cultural beliefs embedded in communication. Thus, the elements of theatrical communication such as language or set pieces no longer appear to be objective, utilitarian or in any sense value-free. The author's or director's or actor's intent ceases to be perceived as a singular enterprise; in so far as it communicates, it works in alliance with the ideology or beliefs of the culture at large.

The notion of encoding shifts the political implications of a theatrical performance from the interpretative sphere of the critic to the signification process of the performance, thereby assigning political alliance to the aesthetic realm. For example, there are cultural encodings in casting-decisions. Juliet, in *Romeo and Juliet*, usually conforms to certain standards of beauty found in the present-day culture. These standards control her costuming and make-up in foregrounding her beauty for the audience. Since Shakespeare wrote the play with a boy actor in mind, the common casting of Juliet does not proceed from the text; rather, it is determined by the cultural encoding inscribed in the image of the female love object. Similarly, the common practice of casting blonde women in the roles of *ingénues*, and dark women in secondary and vamp roles, is not based on the demands of the text, but betrays cultural attitudes about the relative innocence, purity and desirability of certain racial features. The blonde hair and fair skin of the *ingénue* are encoded with these values. The casting of beautiful women in *ingénue* roles, or the rise of the beautiful stage star, participates in patriarchal prejudices that control the sign system of the representation of women on stage.

For feminists, these discoveries help to illuminate how the image of a woman on stage participates directly in the dominant ideology of gender. Social conventions about the female gender will be encoded in all signs for women. Inscribed in body language, signs of gender can determine the blocking of a scene, by assigning bolder movements to the men and more restricted movements to the women, or by creating poses and positions that exploit the role of woman as sexual object. Stage movement replicates the proxemics of the social order, capitalising upon the spatial relationships in the culture at large between women and the sites of power.[3]

Overall, feminist semiotics concentrates on the notion of 'woman as sign'. From this perspective, a live woman standing on the stage is not a biological or natural reality, but 'a fictional construct, a distillate from diverse but congruent discourses dominant in Western cultures'.[4] In other words, the conventions of the stage produce a meaning for the sign 'woman', which is based upon their cultural associations with the female gender. Feminist semiotic theory has attempted to describe and deconstruct this sign for 'woman', in order to distinguish biology from culture and experience from ideology. Whereas formerly feminist criticism presumed to know what a woman is, but rejected certain images of women, this new perspective brings into question the entire notion of how one knows what the sign 'woman' means. At this point, the entire gender category 'woman' is under feminist semiotic deconstruction.

Given the assumption that stage and audience co-produce the performance text, the meaning of the sign 'woman' is also created by the audience. The way the viewer perceives the woman on stage constitutes another theoretical enterprise. In her book *Women and Film*,[5] E. Ann Kaplan characterises this enterprise as 'the male gaze'. Kaplan asserts that the sign 'woman' is constructed by and for the male gaze. In the realm of theatrical production, the gaze is owned by the male: the majority of playwrights, directors and producers are men. This triumvirate determines the nature of the theatrical gaze, deriving the sign for 'woman' from their perspective. In the realm of audience reception, the gaze is encoded with culturally determined components of male sexual desire, perceiving 'woman' as a sexual object. This analysis of the male gaze is informed by feminist psychosemiotics, a combination of post-Lacanian psychoanalysis, semiotics and feminism. The entire argument is too complex and too lengthy to be developed in full here, and the reader is referred to books on feminism semiotics and film by Kaplan, Teresa de Lauretis and Kaja Silverman. However, because of the centrality of this argument to the new understanding of the representation of women, it is necessary to describe certain portions of it in order to suggest the way in which it might serve a feminist poetics of theatre. Since psychosemiotics was developed in film criticism, it must be adapted somewhat if it is to be applied to an analysis of the stage. For instance, whereas in film the principal means of organising the gaze is the camera, a different set of dynamics applies in relation to the stage. Nevertheless, the cultural constitution of the male gaze is essential for most of the performing arts.

The concept of the male gaze asserts that representations of women are perceived as they are seen by men. Here, the term 'men' represents the male subject in capitalist patriarchy. A simple example of how everyone sees a play as a male would see it might be the way a play induces the audience to view the female roles through the eyes of the male characters. When the *ingénue* makes her entrance, the audience sees her as the male protagonist sees her. The blocking of her entrance, her costume and the lighting are designed to reveal that she is the object of his desire. In this way, the audience also perceives her as an object of desire, by identifying with his male gaze. This example illustrates one major cultural assumption – that the male is the subject of the dramatic action. What psychosemiotics establishes is the nature of his subjectivity. This requires the dominant cultural description of the psychological self found in Freud and Lacan. For feminists, Freud and Lacan provide the patriarchal determination of sexual development that explains both the psychosexual male subject and the way that he has come to represent the subject position for the culture at large.

Using Freudian principles, Lacan explains the psychosexual development of the subject in terms of his relationship to symbols. The use of symbols (implying all discourse) is a compensation for the early experience of undifferentiated self-satisfaction. For Lacan, culture intrudes upon libidinal pleasure from the moment the infant begins to identify bodily zones. In other words, in infancy the body feels pleasure anywhere and everywhere – it is the culture which imposes limited erotic zones. Once attuned to cultural laws, the child then perceives that there is something like a self, a discrete unit of identity (Lacan's 'mirror stage'). He trades his earlier, undefined realm of self-satisfaction for the desire to be a self. The self is actually a cultural ideal, alienating him from his libidinal pleasure. The organisation of selfhood then drives him into the symbolic order of the culture. Thus, the subject's participation in the world of symbols is always marked by an alienation from the satisfaction of libidinal desires and the resulting state of unfulfilled desire. For the purposes of analysing performance, this means that the creation of theatre itself springs from the condition of unfulfilled desire in the male subject. He has been denied any real satisfaction and establishes the stage as a site for his alienated, symbolic yearning for satisfaction. This drive towards art determines its system of representation and the nature of the way it produces desire in the viewer.

This entire process excludes women from the role of the subject, or the producer of symbolic expressions. Because it is tied to a cultural castration, both Freud and Lacan locate the symbolic order in relation to the phallus of the child and the cultural 'Law of the Father', situating the entire production of art within the patriarchal order of father and son. Within this order of male desire and castration, the only role for women is as objects of that desire. The result is that women become fixed in the position of object of the gaze, rather than as the subject directing it; women appear in order to be looked upon rather than to do the looking. In that sense, 'woman' is constituted as 'Other'. Concomitantly, she is invested with those qualities which the masculine gazer desires to construct as 'Other' than himself. Thus, women on stage never represent the subject position – their desire is not symbolised in patriarchal culture. Nor do the dynamics of their desire operate within the theatrical experience. The audience becomes the male subject, exiled in the system of theatrical representation and driven by unfulfilled desire. When the audience looks at a woman on stage, she is perceived as a possible site for the fulfilment of that desire, transformed into a kind of cultural courtesan. When pushed to its extremes, this psychosemiotic analysis accounts for the complicity between the stage and pornography.

For women, one of the results of this representation of woman as 'Other' in the male gaze is that she also becomes an 'Other' to herself. Within the patriarchal system of signs, women do not have the cultural mechanisms of meaning to construct themselves as the subject rather than as the object of performance. A wedge is created between the sign 'woman' and real women that insinuates alienation into the very participation of women in the system of theatrical representation or within the system of communication in the dominant culture. This alienation between actual women and the sign 'woman' has already been illustrated in the description of Caryl Churchill's *Cloud Nine* (see Chapter 5). Remember that in Act I, Betty, the wife, is played by a man in drag. Betty is everything men want her to be – the drag role foregrounds her gender as a fiction of the male gaze. There is no real woman under the requirements of costume, make-up and body language. At this point in history, it may be that any representation of 'woman' is tainted by the encoding of that sign within a patriarchal culture. For this reason, some feminist film-makers do not use women as objects of the camera's gaze. Women are represented only by the narrative voice-over, which locates all images on the screen within the female narrative, producing a female subject rather than object of the film.

As demonstrated above, both the study of woman as sign and the study of woman as object are deconstructive strategies that aid in exposing the patriarchal encodings in the dominant system of representation. Yet the potential for women to emerge as subjects rather than objects opens up a field of new possibilities for women in theatre and its system of representation. Constructing woman as subject is the future, liberating work of a feminist new poetics. But, before exploring this work, the term 'subject' needs definition. The subject is a linguistic or philosophical function that can be represented by the pronoun 'I'. The subject represents a point of view. The subject in semiotics is that which controls the field of signs. Moving away from the Cartesian premise 'I think therefore I am', new theories no longer perceive the subject as the discrete basis of experience. Rather, the subject is a position in terms of a linguistic field or an artistic device such as narrative. What had earlier been considered a 'self', a biological or natural entity, imbued with the sense of the 'personal', is now perceived as a cultural construction and a semiotic function. The subject is an intersection of cultural codes and practices.

For feminists, gender is the crucial encoding of the subject that has made it historically a position unavailable for women to inhabit. The traditional subject has been the male subject, with whom everyone must identify. Scanning the 'masterpieces' of the theatre, with their focus on the male subject, one can see that women are called upon to identify with Hamlet, Oedipus, Faust and other male characters imbued with specifically male psychosexual anxieties. The idea that these are 'universal' characters represses the gender inscription in the notion of the self. Yet the dominance of the self as male has taken its historical toll on women, as is evident from women writers who lived in male drag, took male pen names (such as George Sand) and consistently created male protagonists in their works, unable to imagine a woman in the role of the subject of a narrative. Freud's theory of the Oedipal crisis has served to enforce the notion of self as male self. Its dominance in Western thought has securely tied the understanding of sexual development to the male subject. Nancy Chodorow, in her book *Mothering*, dismantles this Freudian model. Illustrating the way in which the girl child has a different dynamic of sexuality and need in the family unit from that of the boy, Chodorow successfully defeats the notions of the Electra complex, derivative of the Oedipal one, and 'penis envy', shifting Freud's focus on the boy to a new focus on the girl.

Nevertheless, the long ascendancy of Freudian psychology universalised his gender-specific theories of development, placing the male in a central subject position and the female in a subordinate, derivative and envious position. Freud's gender-specific notions of psychological development are central to many of the operations of the theatre. For example, they provide the basis of Method acting. The psychological construction of character, using techniques adapted from Stanislavski, places the female actor within the range of systems that have oppressed her very representation on stage. The techniques for the inner construction of a character rely on Freudian principles, leading the female actor into that misogynistic view of female sexuality. In building such characters as Amanda in Tennessee Williams's *Glass Menagerie*, the female actor learns to be passive, weak and dependent in her sexual role, with a fragile inner life that reveals no sexual desire. If one compares this kind of character to Alan Strang in Peter Shaffer's *Equus*, for example, it is easy to see the Freudian blindness to female desire. In *Equus*, the young man's sexuality is blatant and aggressive, giving the male actor a complex and active internal monologue. In his interactions with the psychiatrist, he holds a subject position of developing sexuality. Female characters, when they do have a complex psychological base, are usually frustrated and unfilfilled – like the Electra on whom their complex is based, they wait for the male to take the subject position of action. Their desire is for him to act, they make no attempt to act for their own fulfilment. From Antigone to Blanche Dubois, the female actor works on the passive, broken sexual development of her characters, which isolates them from the social community rather than integrating them into it. From a feminist perspective, the Method techniques for building these characters lead the female actor into inaccurate analyses of female sexuality.

Other acting techniques, such as the playing of an objective and establishing a through line, are also culturally inscribed models from the patriarchal culture. Gillian Hanna of the Monstrous Regiment refers to such linear modes as peculiar to male experience, and insists that her feminist troupe hopes to refute them: 'It's precisely a refusal to accept . . . that life is linear . . . which has to do with male experience. . . . They [men] are born into a world where they can map out life . . . it has to do with a career. It has to do with your work. . . . Now for a woman, life is not like that. It doesn't have that pattern. For a woman life and experience is broken-backed.'[6] Hanna points out that men build a career for life and proceed through school to work in their professions, while women interrupt those processes with child-bearing, child-rearing, and so on. Thus, 'for them life doesn't have that kind of linear overview that it seems to have for men. . . . I think we've been trying to reflect that fragmented experience in what we do.' In other words, objectives and through-lines might not be suitable acting techniques for representing women's experiences. For the female actor to understand a female character, the through-line might be a fallacious way to work. Nevertheless, such work is required by the texts the actors inherit.

Logically, the rejection of these acting techniques implies a rejection of the kind of plays they serve. Playwrights who have been influenced by psychoanalysis both personally and formally have constructed texts that reflect the Freudian perspective on male and female sexual behaviour. A feminist review of the sexuality of Blanche in Williams's *A Streetcar Named Desire*, of the mother in Eugene O'Neill's *Long Day's Journey into Night* or of Rosalyn in Arthur Miller's *The Misfits* could reveal the ways in which these characters were drawn from Freudian biases. Likewise, as may been seen from the relationships between Blanche and Stanley in *Streetcar*, the mother and the father in

Long Day's Journey, and the dancer Rosalyn and cowboy Gay in *The Misfits*, these texts portray women's sexuality as subordinate and derivative in relation to that of the leading male characters, reflecting the subject position of male sexuality within the Freudian-based theatrical domain. Even the formal characteristics of certain genres betray the same values. Realism, in its focus on the domestic sphere and the family unit, reifies the male as sexual subject and the female as the sexual 'Other'. The portrayal of female characters within the family unit – with their confinement to the domestic setting, their dependence on the husband, their often defeatist, determinist view of the opportunities for change – makes realism a 'prisonhouse of art' for women, both in their representation on stage and in the female actor's preparation and production of such roles.

An even deeper analysis which has recently emerged in the realm of feminist psychosemiotics suggests that the form of narrative itself is complicit with the psychocultural repression of women. The film critic Laura Mulvey puts it this way: 'Sadism demands a story, depends on making something happen, forcing a change in another person, a battle of will and strength, victory/defeat, all occurring in a linear time with a beginning and an end.'[7] Mulvey describes the relationship of protagonist and antagonist as sado-masochistic. In her book *Alice Doesn't*, Teresa de Lauretis takes this idea and pushes it to a feminist conclusion: within the typical narrative, the male is the one who makes something happen (the typical hero), who forces a change in another through a battle of wills. He is given the role of the sadist. In love stories, the defeated one is typically the female. Within the narrative structure, the female plays the masochist to the male sadist. Freud has also drawn the character of female sexuality as a masochistic one, locating female masochism in the natural development of the child. The popularity of such stories indicates the sado-masochistic nature of desire in the community at large. The reader or the audience member who gains pleasure from this narrative structure joins in the reification of male and female sexuality as a battle in which the female is defeated. Desire, which propels the story forward, is sadistic and encoded in terms of male and female genders. The structure of narrative as well as its broad appeal enacts this process in the culture.

Portrait of Dora (*Portrait de Dora*, 1976), a play written by

French feminist Hélène Cixous, illustrates the feminist perspective on this psychocultural process. Cixous has long been recognised by the international feminist community as a leading theoretician, especially for her provocative article 'The Laugh of the Medusa', on women and writing.[8] *Dora* was the result of a collaboration with director and playwright Simone Benmussa and is a good example of feminist psychological theory at work on the stage. Reversing the Freudian mandate, Cixous chose to dramatise a case in which Freud was confronted with the sexual development of a female. His attempt to overlay her experiences with his gender-specific theories provides several levels of irony and shifts of perspective in the play. Cixous places a woman in the subject position, revealing Freud's distance from her as an active sexual subject, his attempt to force her into her 'proper' passive, patriarchal position (as she lies on her back on his couch) and his mythologising of her experience. The irony peaks when Dora tries to articulate her attraction to another woman, Mrs K. Freud cannot accommodate this attraction within his theoretical framework. Without a penis, there can be no sex. Therefore, he translates her desire for another woman into a displacement of desire for her father. Freud imposes the Electra complex onto the girl's experience. Instead, the girl exhibits a desire for the mother, a concept also recently developed by Nancy Chodorow in *Mothering*.

Freud continues to misrepresent what Dora tells him, aligning himself with the other men in the play who want to manipulate the girl's sexual development for their own ends. By the end of the play, Dora has rejected all of their impositions, walking off the stage as an independent woman. The final lines suggest that it is Freud who made a transference onto the patient, rather than the traditional, inverse process. The loose frame of the action is the process of psychoanalysis between Freud and Dora, which permits the intrusion of dream, fantasy and memory into the play. On the formal level, the play abandons the conventions of realism. Past, present and fantasy mix freely on stage, with characters coming and going without traditional motivations or playing-moments. Scenes between Dora and Freud and scenes presenting characters from her past occur simultaneously. Sound-effects that convey elements of Dora's subconscious images intrude upon the dialogue. In spite of Freud, Dora becomes the subject of sexuality, fragmenting the elements of her character through the formal devices of the play. The stage becomes a playing-site for Dora's internal images. In her introduction to the published version of the play, Benmussa, who helped to develop the play as well as direct it, describes the stage as analogous to the process of psychoanalysis:

> In 'stage work', just as in 'dream work', a situation, or a desire, is projected into space by a word or a gesture: stage work produces images. Stage is the reflecting surface of a dream, of a deferred dream. It is the meeting place of the desires which . . . both accumulate and cancel each other out as they succeed one another, change their medium, pass from word to gesture, and from image to body. . . . They concentrate a desire very powerfully, but they create around them a nebulous zone which allows the spectator to divine the other, distant, obscure, ever-widening circles in which other desires are lying in wait.[9]

Female desire is the subject, the leading character of this drama.

Benmussa also notes that this play requires something different from the actors. She wants 'to cut the explanatory scenes and retain only the symbols. . . . To leave the actors in danger, as if balancing on the words, balancing on the gestures that filled the gaps between the words; to make the staging more like choreography than like the kind of acting usually considered appropriate to psychological situations.' In other words, the representation of Dora's desire, of female desire, is not trapped within the sado-machochistic dynamics of traditional narrative, or within the traditional representation of such a character as Dora; here, female desire plays freely across the stage in sounds, characters, intersections of fantasy and reality, and even through the role entitled 'the Voice of the Play'. In this way, the form releases the expression of female desire from the snares of patriarchal narrative structures and traditional forms of representation that have repressed woman as subject. Cixous and Benmussa are on their way to creating a new kind of representation of women on stage, reversing the patriarchal order of desire determined by Freudian theories and the male gaze. If, as Benmussa asserts above, the spectator is drawn into this new 'nebulous zone', perhaps the dramaturgical experience of the play operates within the new poetics.

Simone Benmussa is the most prominent woman director to have consistently developed this new psychosemiotic approach to the dramatisation of female desire. Her productions, based on the works of such women writers as Virginia Woolf and Nathalie Sarraute, have played in Paris, London and New York. Her play *The Singular Life of Albert Nobbs* has already been described in Chapter 5. There, its subject matter was treated as an example of the dramatisation of modes of production and a class analysis. Within the present context, the formal devices of the play illustrate her experimentation with the order of representation. While *Dora* represents the liberation of the desiring female subject, *Albert Nobbs* represents the repressive effects of patriarchal culture. Only women appear on stage in this play, from the maids to the concierge. The male characters are invisible, intervening only by voice-overs and mysteriously moving doors. The story of the play is told by the voice of George Moore, the author of the short story from which the play was derived. Moore's voice begins and ends the play, placing the lives of these women within the patriarchal frame of the male creator. By placing all the male characters off stage but making their voices central to the movement of the plot, Benmussa shows that Albert, the woman in drag, and the other women operate within the invisible frame of patriarchal culture, which creates the interactions among women, and even drag itself, from the outside. Within the patriarchal frame, the oppression of the women in the play is opposed to the distant, elite situation of the men. At the same time, the absence of men on stage shifts the dramatic focus to the lives of women and their experiences. Benmussa creates representations of women within the traditional forms of narrative and character development, but foregrounds the patriarchal foundations of such forms.

Women's language and form

The discoveries about the political nature of traditional forms raises the question, 'Is there a women's form – a feminine morphology?' If women are to be the subjects rather than the objects of cultural production, doesn't this cultural revolution necessitate a new form and perhaps even a new discourse for women? This question has produced a major debate within feminist critical theory. Chapter 4 describes the interest of radical feminists in a new vocabulary and forms. Many feminist critics closer to the materialist position would argue that the notion of a feminine form merely reifies the traditional gender constructions of masculine and feminine – that any liberation for women in art would come from their freedom to create in any kind of formal context. Others, closer to the position of the new poetics, would argue that a reorganisation of theories of libidinal development and dramaturgical devices would create a new position for the female desiring subject that would change the way the field of signs is constructed. Lacan's new compound of the Oedipal crisis and the acquisition of symbols has become a major catalyst in feminist theories of women and cultural forms.

Cixous's essay 'The Laugh of the Medusa' is a central text in the call for a new form. Cixous relates the fact that there have been few women writers to the notion that, culturally, women's bodies have been assimilated by the patriarchal system of desire and representation. Cixous calls on women to reclaim their bodies and their writing, establishing a reciprocal relationship between the two:

> By writing her self, woman will return to the body which has been more than confiscated from her, which has been turned into the uncanny stranger on display – the ailing or dead figure, which so often turns out to be the nasty companion, the cause and location of inhibitions. Censor the body and you censor breath and speech at the same time. Write your self. Your body must be heard.[10]

Cixous then describes what this new women's language, written from her body, will be like. The writing will be heterogenous and far-ranging: 'Woman un-thinks the unifying, regulating history that homogenizes and channels forces, herding contradictions into a single battlefield.' In some ways, Cixous's position resembles Mary Daly's radical-feminist notion of 'Spinsters'. It also resembles Gillian Hanna's characterisation of male plays, and the Monstrous Regiment's search for a new form proceeding from women's experiences. Hanna characterises the male dramatic form as 'a sweep of history, something broad and heavy . . . the male playwright's sensitivity is often like an empire builder – it wants to consume the whole world and then spit it out again in its own image'.[11]

The term that emerges in many articles concerning a new, feminine morphology is 'contiguity'. This is an organisational device that feminists have discovered in both early and modern works by women. Luce Irigaray describes it as a 'nearness', creating a form 'constantly in the process of weaving itself . . . embracing words and yet casting them off', concerned not with clarity, but with what is 'touched upon'.[12] Cixous calls it 'working the in-between', and Jane Gallop describes it as 'the register of touching, nearness, presence, immediacy, contact'.[13] It can be elliptical rather than illustrative, fragmentary rather than whole, ambiguous rather than clear, and interrupted rather than complete. This contiguity exists within the text and at its borders: the feminine form seems to be without a sense of formal closure – in fact, it operates as an anti-closure. Cixous describes it this way: 'Her language does not contain, it carries; it does not hold back, it makes possible', signifying 'the erotogeneity of the heterogeneous'.[14] Without closure, the sense of beginning, middle and end, or a central focus, it abandons the hierarchical organising-principles of traditional form that served to elide women from discourse. Women can inhabit the realm of the outsider – in Lacan's system, the one who 'lacks the lack' – and create a new discourse and form that exhibit the field of female experience.

Within the study of the theatre, several versions of masculine and feminine morphology have taken hold. For example, some feminist critics have described the form of tragedy as a replication of the male sexual experience. Tragedy is composed of foreplay, excitation and ejaculation (catharsis). The broader organisation of plot – complication, crisis and resolution – is also tied to this phallic experience. The central focus in male forms is labelled phallocentric, reflecting the nature of the male's sexual physiology. A female form might embody her sexual mode, aligned with multiple orgasms, with no dramatic focus on ejaculation or necessity to build to a single climax. The contiguous organisation would replace this ejaculatory form. The feminist critic might analyse the plays of Adrienne Kennedy, women's performance-art pieces or witches' cyclic rituals using this notion.

The opponents of this kind of thinking point out that what begins to emerge in this idea of feminine morphology is the sense that the female gender is real, rather than an invention of the patriarchy. Moreover, gender has been biologised – the notions of the female body and the male body have been used to re-create the dominant cultural systems of representation. Instead, these opponents argue, it would be better to realise that 'One is not Born a Woman' (the title of Monique Wittig's influential anti-gender article). The concept of a feminine morphology retains the traditional inscription of gender onto cultural forms, merely inverting the value system. Critics such as Wittig argue that, by valorising the feminine, feminists will keep women in the ghetto of gender. Some theatre practitioners have also responded negatively to the notion of feminine form. They feel it means that, if they work in traditional forms, they are not feminists (or feminine), and that their work is discounted because of their preference for those forms, rather than seen as marking an advance for women in the field by making their professional work visible.

Feminist critics who prescribe a feminine form have been termed 'essentialists' by their opponents. This means that they ignore the economic and historical conditions that have determined the process of cultural gender inscription. They are termed essentialists to contrast them with materialists, who emphasise the economic and historical advantages of gender inscription for the elite class of men in the patriarchy. To associate this process with biology is to subscribe to biological determinism, ignoring the contradictions and processes of history, such as class and race. In other words, the proposed feminine morphology would fall within the category of radical-feminist thought and be fundamentally opposed to materialist feminism. Instead, materialist creators prefer to explore non-gendered roles, behaviour and texts (see, for example, the description of Zeig's and Wittig's experiments in acting techniques, in Chapter 4).

It seems, however, that certain gains can be realised from both sides of the issue. Perhaps these positions could be combined in some way, or, within a historical context, perceived as alternative theoretical strategies for specific political purposes. They need not operate as competing theories for a controlling position that subsumes practice and organises positions, much like the theoretical strategies operating in the 'Name of the Father'. Rather, they would appear as tactics to be employed when they were useful in either dismantling the patriarchal structure or aiding in the cultural revolution. Theory would then be in the service of specific politic manoeuvres rather than rising to a transcendent position. Retaining theory in a dialectical partnership with practice is one way to alleviate the anxieties among feminists that it is elitist. If a theory does not assume a transcendent posture, it can be used for the politics of the moment, adapted by them, and repeatedly altered or forsaken in different historical and political situations. The feminist activist–theorist can employ any techniques, methods, theories or ways of social organising she wishes in confronting or creating the situations in which she operates.

The arguments for and against a feminine morphology produce different political effects in different situations. For example, a feminist critic working in a conservative academic environment might make use of a feminine morphology to contradict the patriarchal valorisation of realism or other traditional forms. When used as a provocation, this morphological notion could invoke a defence of the traditional codes, raising questions concerning the canon and the structure of dramatic interpretation within the parameters of an alternative, feminist tradition. Again, such a morphology might provide a way to push for a re-evaluation of women's work in the theatre, both by demonstrating the existence of a distinctively feminine form and by exposing the bastions of male privilege in the arts as political defences against it. The feminist critic, then, would no longer be cast in the negative role of the gadfly, or in the role of one on the defensive against the *status quo*, but would appear as the proponent of a new theory and an alternative practice.

On the other hand, in dialogue with feminists who valorise the gender inscription in the feminine morphology, the same critic might utilise the materialist analysis of form. In this case, she could raise the issues of race and class which are so important to the understanding and reception of works by women of colour and working-class women, and which have such a strong bearing on their relationship to the theatre. Here she could note their absence from many avant-garde formalist experiments, as well as the absence of a historical context. By employing alternative theories at different times, the feminist critic would still remain firmly within the operations of the feminist movement, which has no leaders, no central organisation and no 'party line'. Swinging from theory to opposing theory as described here would not be a kind of 'playful pluralism', but a guerrilla action designed to provoke and focus the feminist critique.

In the theatre, the new poetics offers the feminist a blend of activism and theoretical practice. With the deconstruction of the forms of representation, and dialogue and modes of perception characteristic of patriarchal culture, the stage can be prepared for the entrance of the female subject, whose voice, sexuality and image have yet to be dramatised within the dominant culture. At this point in history, psychosemiotic strategies may provide a new kind of revolution, for in the late twentieth century the mode of production which is central to the oppression of many peoples lies within the ghettoes of signs and codes. In the age of television, computer languages and communication satellites, the production of signs creates the sense of what a person is, rather than reflects it (in the traditional mimetic order). The mode of cultural production is reversed: signs create reality rather than reflect it. This condition means that artists and cultural theorists may be the activists and the revolutionaries. Modes of discourse and representation may replace the Molotov cocktail.

The feminist in theatre can create the laboratory in which the single most effective mode of repression – gender – can be exposed, dismantled and removed; the same laboratory may produce the representation of a subject who is liberated from the repressions of the past and capable of signalling a new age for both women and men.

Notes

Chapter 1. Traditional History: A Feminist Deconstruction

1. Margarete Bieber, *The History of the Greek and Roman Theatre* (Princeton, NJ: Princeton University Press, 1939) p. 9.
2. See Gayle Rubin, 'The Traffic in Women: Notes on the "Political Economy" of Sex', in Rayna R. Reiter (ed.), *Toward an Anthropology of Women*, (New York: Monthly Review, 1975), for a discussion of women as a medium of exchange through the institution of marriage and kinship laws.
3. Marilyn Arthur, '"Liberated" Women: The Classical Era', in Renate Bridenthal and Claudia Koonz (eds), *Becoming Visible: Women in European History* (Boston, Mass.: Houghton Mifflin, 1977) pp. 67–8.
4. Nancy Hartsock, *Money, Sex and Power: Toward a Feminist Historical Materialism* (New York: Longman, 1983) p. 187.
5. Page du Bois, *Centaurs and Amazons* (Ann Arbor: University of Michigan Press, 1982) p. 2.
6. William Blake Tyrrell, *Amazons: A Study in Athenian Mythmaking* (Baltimore: Johns Hopkins University Press, 1984) p. 47.
7. Ibid., p. 55.
8. Plato, in Edith Hamilton and Huntington Cairns (eds), *The Collected Dialogues* (New York: Bollingen Foundation/Pantheon Books, 1961) p. 855.
9. Bieber, *History of the Greek and Roman Theatre*, p. 1.
10. Ibid., p. 9.
11. Hartsock, *Money, Sex and Power*, p. 192.
12. Ibid., p. 198.
13. All quotations from *The Oresteia* are from *The Complete Greek Tragedies, Aeschylus*, ed. David Greene and Richmond Lattimore (Chicago: University of Chicago Press, 1960). Line references are given.
14. Sir Arthur Pickard-Cambridge, *The Dramatic Festivals of Athens* (Oxford: Clarendon Press, 1968) p. 265.
15. Quoted from *Aristotle's Poetics*, ed. O. B. Hardison, Tr. Leon Golden (Englewood Cliffs, NJ: Prentice-Hall, 1968). Subsequently identified as 'Golden', to distinguish from the translation by Else (see following note), with line references following quotations.

16. Quoted from *Aristotle's Poetics: The Argument*, tr. and ed. Gerald F. Else (Cambridge, Mass.: Harvard University Press, 1963). Subsequently identified as 'Else', to distinguish from the translation by Golden (see preceding note), with line references following quotations.

17. Quoted in Mary Lefkowitz and Maureen B. Fant, *Women's Life in Greece and Rome* (Baltimore: Johns Hopkins University Press, 1982) p. 64.

18. Ibid.

19. Glynne Wickham, *Early English Stages*, vol. I (New York: Columbia University Press, 1959) p. 252.

20. See Carole Vance, Introduction to Ann Snitow, Christine Stansell and Sharon Thompson (eds), *Powers of Desire: The Politics of Sexuality* (New York: Monthly Review, 1983) p. 4.

21. Quoted from Lisa Jardine, *Still Harping on Daughters* (Totowa, NJ: Barnes and Noble, 1983) p. 40.

22. Ibid., p. 20.

23. Harley Granville-Barker, *Prefaces to Shakespeare*, vol. I (Princeton, NJ: Princeton University Press, 1952) p. 15.

24. Johann Wolfgang von Goethe, *Goethe's Travels in Italy*, tr. and ed. Charles Lisbeth (London: 1883) pp. 433–4.

25. Jan Kott, *Shakespeare our Contemporary*, tr. Boleslaw Taborski (London: Methuen, 1965).

26. Marianne L. Novy, *Love's Argument: Gender Relations in Shakespeare* (Chapel Hill, NC, and London: University of North Carolina Press, 1984) p. 200.

27. Luce Irigaray, 'When the Goods Get Together', in Elaine Marks and Isabelle de Courtivron (eds), *New French Feminisms* (New York: Schocken Books, 1981) p. 107.

Chapter 2. Women Pioneers

1. All quotations from Hrotsvit taken from *The Plays of Roswitha*, tr. Christopher St John (London: Chatto and Windus, 1923).

2. For new treatments of Hrotsvit, see A. Daniel Frankforter, 'Sexism and the Search for Thematic Structure of the Plays of Hroswitha of Gandersheim', *International Journal of Women's Studies*, 2.3 (1979); and Sue-Ellen Case, 'Re-Viewing Hrotsvit', *Theatre Journal*, Dec. 1983.

3. Maureen Duffy, *The Passionate Shepherdess* (London: Jonathan Cape, 1977) p. 158.

4. Virginia Woolf, *A Room of One's Own* (New York: Harcourt, Brace and World, 1929) p. 67.

5. Duffy, *The Passionate Shepherdess*, p. 158.

6. Ibid., p. 248.

7. Nancy Cotton, *Women Playwrights in England, 1363–1750* (London: Associated University Presses, 1980) pp. 16–21.

8. Susanna Centlivre, *The Works of the Celebrated Mrs Centlivre*, vol. I (London: J. Knapton, 1949) pp. 217–18.
9. For a more extended discussion, see Mary Fullerton, 'Susannah Centlivre' (unpublished essay, University of Washington School of Drama, 1983).
10. Sor Juana, *The Reply*, tr. Margaret Sayers Peden in *A Woman of Genius* (Salisbury: Lime Rock, 1982), p. 39.
11. Octavio Paz, *Sor Juana Inés de la Cruz o las trampas le la fé* (Mexico: Fondo de Cultura Economica, 1982); and Estela Portillo Trambley, *Sor Juana and Other Plays* (Michigan: Bilingual Press/Editorial Bilingüe, 1983).
12. Alice Robinson, 'Mercy Warren, Satirist of the Revolution', in Helen Krich Chinoy and Linda Walsh Jenkins (eds), *Women in American Theatre* (New York: Crown, 1981) p. 133.
13. See preceding note.

Chapter 3. Personal Theatre

1. This concept of salon as women's theatre is derived from an article by Helen Fehervary, 'Christa Wolf's Prose: A Landscape of Masks', *New German Critique*, 27 (Fall 1982).
2. Kay Goodman, 'Poesis and Praxis in Rahel Varnhagen's Letters', ibid., p. 126.
3. Ibid., p. 131.
4. Ibid., p. 132.
5. Ibid.
6. Georges Wickes, *The Amazon of Letters: The Life and Loves of Natalie Barney* (New York: Popular Library, 1978); and Jean Chalon, *Portrait of a Seductress* (New York: Crown, 1979).
7. Joan Schenkar, *Natalie Barney* (unpublished playscript, 1984).
8. Wickes, *The Amazon of Letters*, p. 92.
9. Chinoy and Jenkins, *Women in American Theatre*, p. 10.
10. Ibid., p. 1.
11. Moira Roth (ed.), *The Amazing Decade: Women in Performance Art 1970–1980* (Los Angeles: Astro Artz, 1983).
12. Quoted in Jeanie K. Forte, 'Rachel Rosenthal: Feminism in Performance Art'. *Women and Performance*, 2.2 (1985) p. 30.
13. See Forte, 'Rachel Rosenthal: Feminism in Performance Art' (preceding note); and for a fuller development of feminism and performance art see Forte's 'Women in Performance Art: Feminism and Postmodernism' (unpublished dissertation, University of Washington, 1986).

Chapter 4. Radical Feminism and Theatre

1. Alison M. Jaggar, *Feminist Politics and Human Nature* (Totowa, NJ: Rowman and Allanheld, 1983) p. 84.

2. For instance, 'Women's Theatre Groups', *Drama Review*, June 1972, pp. 79–84; and 'Women for Women', *Drama Review*, Dec. 1974, pp. 77–87.
3. See 'Women for Women', *Drama Review*, Dec. 1974.
4. Michelene Wandor, *Understudies: Theatre and Sexual Politics* (London: Methuen, 1981) p. 24.
5. Readers interested in further research in this field may refer to Rosemary Curb's 'Catalog of Feminist Theater' in *Chrysalis*, 10 (1979); Dinah Louise Leavitt's *Feminist Theatre Groups* (1980); 'Acting Up: Women in Theatre and Performance', a special issue of *Heresies* (Fall 1984); and Elie Natalle's *Feminist Theatre* (1985).
6. Mary Daly, *Gyn/Ecology* (Boston, Mass.: Beacon Press, 1978) p. 386.
7. Susan Griffin, *Women and Nature: The Roaring Inside Her* (New York: Harper Colophon, 1980) p. 226.
8. Z. Budapest, *The Feminist Book of Lights and Shadows* (Venice, Calif.: The Feminist Wicca, 1975) pp. 1–2.
9. Charlene Spretnak (ed.), *The Politics of Women's Spirituality* (Garden City, NY: Anchor Books, 1982) p. 53.
10. Ibid., p. 54.
11. Budapest, *The Feminist Book of Lights and Shadows*, p. 11.
12. Spretnak, *The Politics of Women's Spirituality*, p. 80.
13. Ibid., p. 469.
14. Budapest, *The Feminist Book of Lights and Shadows*, pp. 67–8.
15. Karen Malpede, *Women in Theatre: Compassion and Hope* (New York: Drama Book Specialists, 1983) p. 255.
16. Starhawk, *The Spiral Dance: A Rebirth of the Ancient Religion of the Great Goddess* (San Francisco: Harper, 1979) p. 79.
17. Dinah Luise Leavitt, *Feminist Theatre Groups* (Jefferson, NC: McFarland, 1980) p. 53.
18. Spretnak, *The Politics of Women's Spirituality*, pp. 317–20.
19. Adrienne Rich, 'Compulsory Heterosexuality and Lesbian Existence', in Snitow *et al.*, *Powers of Desire*, p. 178.
20. Alison Jaggar and Paula Rothenberg (eds), *Feminist Frameworks* (New York: McGraw-Hill, 1984) p. 156.
21. Kate McDermott (ed.), *Places Please! The First Anthology of Lesbian Plays* (n.p.: Aunt Lute Book Co., 1985).
22. Harriet Ellenberger, 'The Dream is the Bridge: In Search of Lesbian Theatre', *Trivia*, 5 (Fall 1984) pp. 26–31.
23. Sande Zeig, 'The Actor as Activator: Deconstructing Gender Through Gesture', *Woman and Performance*, 2.2 (1985) p. 14.
24. Ibid., p. 16.
25. See Jill Dolan, 'Women's Theatre Program ATA: Creating a Feminist Forum', *Woman and Performance*, 1.2 (1984); and the major discussion of her theories in 'Toward a Critical Methodology of Lesbian Feminist Theatre' (unpublished master's thesis, New York University, 1983).

Chapter 5. Materialist Feminism

1. All quotations are from Dario Fo and Franca Rame, *Female Parts: One-Woman Plays*, adaptation by Olwen Wymark, tr. Margaret Kunzle and Stuart Hood (London: Pluto Press, 1981). Another version was adapted, translated and performed by Estelle Parsons, 1983, under the title *Orgasmo Adulto Escapes From the Zoo*; unpublished, but discussed in an interview with Parsons in *Women and Performance*, 2.1 (1984) pp. 49–62.
2. Gillian Hanna, 'Feminism and Theatre', *Theatre Papers*, 2nd ser., no. 8 (Dartington, Devon: Dartington College, 1978) p. 3.

Chapter 6. Women of Colour and Theatre

1. See Yvonne Yarbro-Bejarano, 'The Image of the Chicana in Teatro', in J. Cochran, J. T. Stewart and M. Tsutakawa (eds), *Gathering Ground: New Writing and Art by Northwest Women of Color* (Seattle: Seal Press, 1984), and 'Chicanas Experience in Collective Theater', *Women and Performance*, 2.2 (1985), in addition to other articles by her cited in this chapter.
2. This is not to deny the historical role of activism for women, obscured in both dominant and Chicano histories.
3. Elizabeth Hadley Freydberg, 'Black Women and Feminism: One More Time (How Many More Times?)', *Theatre News*, Fall 1981, p. 22.
4. Audre Lorde, 'The Uses of Anger: Women Responding to Racism', *Sister Outsider* (Trumansburg, NY: The Crossing, 1984) pp. 128–30.
5. Beah E. Richards, *A Black Woman Speaks and Other Poems* (Los Angeles: Inner City Press, 1974) p. 32.
6. *Narratives: A Dramatic Event* (New York: Kitchen Table Women of Color Press, 1983).
7. Clare Venables, 'The Woman Director in the Theatre', *Theatre Quarterly*, Summer 1980.
8. Yvonne Yarbro-Bejarano, 'The Role of Women in Chicano Theater Organizations', *El Tecolote Literary Magazine* (San Francisco) 2.3–4 (Dec. 1981).
9. Ibid.
10. Yvonne Yarbro-Bejarano, '*Teatropoesia* by Chicanas in the Bay Area: *Tongues of Fire*', *Revista Chicano-Requena*, XI.1 (1983) p. 79.
11. Ibid., p. 85.
12. Ibid., p. 81.
13. Performance Programme, Spiderwoman Theatre, 1983.
14. Cochran *et al.*, *Gathering Ground*.

Chapter 7. Towards a New Poetics

1. Carolyn Allen, 'Feminism and Postmodernism', in Joseph Natoli (ed.), *Tracing Literary Theory* (forthcoming).

2. Keir Elam, *The Semiotics of Theatre and Drama* (London: Methuen, 1980) p. 1.
3. See Nancy Henley, *Body Politics* (Englewood Cliffs, NJ: Prentice-Hall, 1977).
4. Teresa de Lauretis, *Alice Doesn't: Feminism, Semiotics and Cinema* (Bloomington: Indiana University Press, 1984) p. 5.
5. E. Ann Kaplan, *Women and Film* (New York: Methuen, 1981) p. 23.
6. Hanna, 'Feminism and Theatre', *Theatre Papers*, 2nd ser., no. 8, p. 8.
7. Laura Mulvey, 'Visual Pleasure and Narrative Cinema', *Screen*, 16.3 (1975) p. 14.
8. Hélène Cixous, 'The Laugh of the Medusa', in Marks and de Courtivron, *New French Feminisms*, pp. 245–64.
9. Simone Benmussa, *Benmussa Directs* (London: John Calder, 1979) p. 9.
10. Cixous, 'The Laugh of the Medusa', in Marks and de Courtivron, *New French Freminisms*, p. 250.
11. Hanna, in *Theatre Papers*, 2nd ser., no. 8, p. 8.
12. Luce Irigaray, 'This Sex Which Is Not One', in Marks and de Courtivron, *New French Feminisms*, pp. 99–106.
13. Jane Gallop, *The Daughter's Seduction: Feminism and Psychoanalysis* (Ithaca, NY: Cornell University Press, 1982) p. 30.
14. Cixous, 'The Laugh of the Medusa', in Marks and de Courtivron, *New French Feminisms*, p. 252.

Bibliography

Chapter 1. Traditional History: A Feminist Deconstruction

Aristotle's Poetics, ed. O. B. Hardison, tr. Leon Golden (Englewood Cliffs, NJ: Prentice-Hall, 1968).

Aristotle's Poetics: The Argument, tr. and ed. Gerald F. Else (Dambridge, Mass.: Harvard University Press, 1963).

Arthur, Marilyn, ' "Liberated" Women: The Classical Era', in Renate Bridenthal and Claudia Koonz (eds), *Becoming Visible: Women in European History* (Boston, Mass.: Houghton Mifflin, 1977).

Bieber, Margarete, *The History of The Greek and Roman Theatre* (Princeton, NJ: Princeton University Press, 1939).

du Bois, Page, *Centaurs and Amazons* (Ann Arbor: University of Michigan Press, 1982).

Fetterley, Judith, *The Resisting Reader: A Feminist Approach to American Fiction* (Bloomington: Indiana University Press, 1978).

Granville-Barker, Harley, *Prefaces to Shakespeare* (Princeton, NJ: Princeton University Press, 1952), vol. I.

Hartsock, Nancy, *Money, Sex and Power: Toward a Feminist Historical Materialism* (New York: Longman, 1983).

Irigaray, Luce. 'When the Goods Get Together', in Elaine Marks and Isabelle de Courtivron (eds), *New French Feminisms* (New York: Schocken, 1981).

Jardine, Lisa, *Still Harping on Daughters* (Totowa, NJ: Barnes and Noble, 1983).

Kelly, Joan, *Women, History, and Theory* (Chicago: University of Chicago Press, 1984).

Kott, Jan, *Shakespeare our Contemporary*, tr. Boleslaw Taborski (London: Methuen, 1965).

Lefkowitz, Mary, and Fant, Maureen B., *Women's Life in Greece and Rome* (Baltimore: Johns Hopkins University Press, 1982).

Millett, Kate, *Sexual Politics* (New York: 1970).

Novy, Marianne L., *Love's Argument: Gender Relations in Shakespeare* (Chapel Hill, NC, and London: University of North Carolina Press, 1984).

Pickard-Cambridge, Sir Arthur, *The Dramatic Festivals of Athens* (Oxford: Clarendon Press, 1968).

Rubin, Gayle, 'The Traffic in Women: Notes on the "Political Economy" of Sex', in Rayna R. Reiter (ed.), *Toward an Anthropology of Women* (New York: Monthly Review, 1975).

Tyrrell, William Blake, *Amazons: A Study in Athenian Mythmaking* (Baltimore: Johns Hopkins University Press, 1984).

Vance, Carole, Introduction to Ann Snitow, Christine Stansell and Sharon Thompson (eds), *Powers of Desire: The Politics of Sexuality* (New York: Monthly Review, 1983).

Wickham, Glynne, *Early English Stages* (New York: Columbia University Press, 1959) vol. I.

Chapter 2. Women Pioneers

Behn, Aphra, *The Works of Aphra Behn*, ed. Montague Summers, 6 vols (London: Heinemann, 1915).

Case, Sue-Ellen, 'Re-viewing Hrotsvit', *Theatre Journal*, Dec 1983.

Centlivre, Susanna, *The Works of the Celebrated Mrs Centlivre*, 3 vols (London: J. Knapton, 1949). Reprint of 1761 ed.

Cotton, Nancy, *Women Playwrights in England, 1363–1750* (London: Associated University Presses, 1980).

Duffy, Maureen, *The Passionate Shepherdess* (London: Jonathan Cape, 1977).

Frankforter, A. Daniel, 'Sexism and the Search for Thematic Structure of the Plays of Hroswitha of Gandersheim', *International Journal of Women's Studies*, 2.3 (1979).

Fullerton, Mary, 'Susanna Centlivre' (unpublished essay, University of Washington School of Drama, 1983).

Hrotsvit (Roswitha), *The Plays of Roswitha*, tr. Christopher St John (London: Chatto and Windus, 1923).

Mason, Louise, 'The Fight to be an American Woman and a Playwright' (unpublished dissertation, University of California at Berkeley, 1983).

Morgan, Fidelis, *The Female Wits* (London: Virago, 1981).

Paz, Octavio, *Sor Juana Inés de la Cruz a las trampas de la fé* (Mexico: Fondo de Cultura Economica, 1982).

Robinson, Alice, 'Mercy Warren, Satirist of the Revolution', in Helen Krich Chinoy and Linda Walsh Jenkins (eds), *Women in American Theatre* (New York: Crown, 1981).

Sor Juana, *The Reply*, tr. Margaret Sayers Peden in *A Woman of Genius* (Salisbury: Lime Rock, 1982).

Trambley, Estela Portillo, *Sor Juana and Other Plays* (Michigan: Bilingual Press/Editorial Bilingüe, 1983).

Warren, Mercy Otis, *The Plays and Poems of Mercy Otis Warren* (New York: Scholars' Facsimiles and Reprints, 1980).

Chapter 3. Personal Theatre

Chalon, Jean, *Portrait of a Seductress* (New York: Crown, 1979).

Chinoy, Helen Krich, and Jenkins, Linda Walsh (eds), *Women in American Theatre* (New York: Crown, 1981).

Fehervary, Helen, 'Christa Wolf's Prose: A Landscape of Masks', *New German Critique*, 27 (Fall 1982) pp. 57–88.

Forte, Jeanie K., 'Rachel Rosenthal: Feminism in Performance Art', *Women and Performance*, 2.2 (1985).

——, 'Women in Performance Art: Feminism and Postmodernism' (unpublished dissertation, University of Washington, 1986).

Goodman, Kay, 'Poesis and Praxis in Rahel Varnhagen's Letters', *New German Critique*, 27 (Fall 1982) pp. 123–40.

Roth, Moira (ed.), *The Amazing Decade: Women and Performance Art in America 1970–1980* (Los Angeles: Astro Artz, 1983).

Schenkar, Joan, *Natalie Barney* (unpublished playscript, 1984).

Wickes, George, *The Amazon of Letters: The Life and Loves of Natalie Barney* (New York: Popular Library, 1978).

Chapter 4. Radical Feminism and Theatre

'Acting Up! Women in Theater and Performance', *Heresies*, special issue (1984).

Budapest, Z., *The Feminist Book of Lights and Shadows* (Venice, Calif.: The Feminist Wicca, 1975).

Chambers, Jane, *Last Summer at Blue Fish Cove* (New York: JH Press, 1982).

——, *Quintessential Image* (unpublished playscript, 1983).

Churchill, Caryl, *Vinegar Tom*, in *Plays by Women*, ed. Michelene Wandor (London: Methuen, 1982) vol. I.

Curb, Rosemary, 'Catalog of Feminist Theatre', *Chrysalis*, 10 (1979).

Daly, Mary, *Gyn/Ecology* (Boston, Mass.: Beacon Press, 1978).

Dolan, Jill, 'Women's Theatre program ATA: Creating a Feminist Forum?', *Women and Performance*, 1.2 (1984) pp. 5–13.

——, 'Toward a Critical Methodology of Lesbian Feminist Theatre' (unpublished master's thesis, New York University, 1984).

Dunn, Nell, *Steaming* (Ambergate, Derbys: Amber Lane Press, 1981).

Echols, Alice, 'The New Feminism of Yin and Yang', in Snitow *et al.*, *Powers of Desire: The Politics of Sexuality*.

Ellenberger, Harriet, 'The Dream is the Bridge: In Search of Lesbian Theatre', *Trivia*, 5 (Fall 1984).

Griffin, Susan, *Women and Nature: The Roaring Inside Her* (New York: Harper, 1980).

Jagger, Alison M., *Feminist Politics and Human Nature* (Totowa, NJ: Rowman and Allanheld, 1983).

Jaggar, Alison, and Rothenberg, Paula (eds), *Feminist Frameworks* (New York: McGraw-Hill, 1984).

Keyssar, Helene, *Feminist Theatre* (London: Macmillan, 1984).

Lamb, Myrna, *But What Have You Done for Me Lately? The Mod Donna and Seyklon 2. Plays of Women's Liberation* (New York: Pathfinder, 1971).

Leavitt, Dinah Luise, *Feminist Theatre Groups* (Jefferson, NC: McFarland, 1980).

Malpede, Karen, *Women in Theatre: Compassion and Hope* (New York: Drama Book Specialists, 1983).
McDermott, Kate (ed.), *Places Please! The First Anthology of Lesbian Plays* (n.p.: Aunt Lute Book Co., 1985).
Natalle, Elie, *Feminist Theatre* (Scarecrow Press, 1985).
Rich, Adrienne, 'Compulsory Heterosexuality and Lesbian Existence', in Snitow *et al.*, *Powers of Desire: The Politics of Sexuality*.
Shange, Ntozake, *for colored girls who have considered suicide when the rainbow is enuf* (New York: Bantam, 1980).
——, *Three Pieces* (New York: St Martin's Press, 1981).
Snitow, Ann, with Stansell, Christine, and Thompson, Sharon (eds), *Powers of Desire: The Politics of Sexuality* (New York: Monthly Review, 1983).
Spretnak, Charlene (ed.), *The Politics of Women's Spirituality* (Garden City, NY: Anchor Books, 1982).
Starhawk, *The Spiral Dance: A Rebirth of the Ancient Religion of the Great Goddess* (San Francisco: Harper, 1979).
Wandor, Michelene, *Understudies: Theatre and Sexual Politics* (London: Methuen, 1981).
Wasserstein, Wendy, *Uncommon Women and Others* (New York: Avon Books, 1978).
Zeig, Sande, 'The Actor as Activator: Deconstructing Gender Through Gesture', *Women and Performance* 1.2 (1984).
Zeig, Sande, and Wittig, Monique, *Lesbian Peoples: Material for a Dictionary* (New York: Avon Books, 1979).

Chapter 5. Materialist Feminism and Theatre

Benmussa, Simone, *The Singular Life of Albert Nobbs*, in *Benmussa Directs* (London: John Calder, 1979).
Churchill, Caryl, *Cloud Nine* (London: Methuen, 1984).
——, *Top Girls* (London: Methuen, 1984).
Gems, Pam, *Dusa, Fish, Stas and Vi*, in *Plays by Women*, ed. Michelene Wandor (London: Methuen, 1982) vol. i.
Hanna, Gillian, 'Feminism and Theatre', *Theatre Papers*, 2nd ser., no. 8 (Dartington, Devon: Dartington College, 1978).
Rame, Franca, and Fo, Dario, *Female Parts*, adapted by Olwen Wymark, tr. Margaret Kunzle and Stuart Hood (London: Pluto, 1982).
Reinshagen, Gerlind, *Eisenherz* (Frankfurt: Suhrkamp Verlag, 1981). (Unpublished English translation by Sue-Ellen Case and Arelene Teraoka, Seattle, Wash., 1983).
Roth, Friederike, *Ritt auf die Wartburg* (Frankfurt: Verlag der Autoren, 1983).
Wandor, Michelene, *Understudies: Theatre and Sexual Politics* (London: Methuen, 1981).

Chapter 6. Women of Colour and Theatre

Childress, Alice, *Florence*, in *Masses and Mainstream* (New York: 1950).
——, *Trouble in Mind*, in *Black Theater*, comp. Lindsay Patterson (New York: Dodd, Mead, 1971).
Cochran, J., Stewart, J. T. and Tsutakawa, M. (eds), *Gathering Ground: New Writing and Art by Northwest Women of Colour* (Seattle: Seal, 1984).
Freydberg, Elizabeth Hadley, 'Black Women and Feminism: One More Time (How Many More Times?)', *Theatre News*, 22 (Fall 1981).
Hill, Erroll, *Shakespeare in Sable: A History of Black Shakespearean Actors* (Amherst: University of Massachusetts Press, 1984).
Hooks, Bell, *From Margin to Center* (Boston, Mass.: South End, 1984).
Kennedy, Adrienne, *The Owl Answers*, in *Cities in Bezique* (New York: Samuel French, 1969).
Lorde, Audre, 'The Uses of Anger: Women Responding to Racism', *Sister Outsider* (Trumansburg, NY: The Crossing, 1984).
Narratives: A Dramatic Event (New York: Kitchen Table Women of Color Press, 1983).
Venables, Clare, 'The Woman Director in the Theatre', *Theatre Quarterly*, Summer 1980.
Richards, Beah E., *A Black Woman Speaks and Other Poems* (Los Angeles: Inner City Press, 1974).
Yarbro-Bejarano, Yvonne, 'Chicanas' Experience in Collective Theater', *Women and Performance*, 2.2 (1985).
——, 'The Role of Women in Chicano Theater Organization', *El Tecolote Literary Magazine*, 2.3–4 (Dec 1981).
——, '*Teatropoesia* by Chicanas in the Bay Area: *Tongues of Fire*', *Revista Chicano-Requena*, XI.1 (1983).

Chapter 7. Towards a New Poetics

Allen, Carolyn, 'Feminism and Postmodernism', in Joseph Natoli (ed.) *Trading Literary Theory* (forthcoming).
Chodorow, Nancy, *The Reproduction of Mothering: Psychoanalysis and the Sociology of Gender* (Berkeley, Calif.: University of California Press, 1978).
Cixous, Hélène, 'The Laugh of the Medusa', in Marks and de Courtivron, *New French Feminisms*.
——, *Portrait of Dora*, in *Benmussa Directs* (London: John Calder, 1978).
de Lauretis, Teresa, *Alice Doesn't: Feminism, Semiotics and Cinema* (Bloomington: Indiana University Press, 1984).
Elam, Keir. *The Semiotics of Theatre and Drama* (London: Methuen, 1980).
Gallop, Jane. *The Daughter's Seduction: Feminism and Psychoanalysis* (Ithaca, NY: Cornell University Press, 1982).

Hanna, Gillian, 'Feminism and Theatre', *Theatre Papers*, 2nd ser. no. 8, (Dartington, Devon: Dartington College, 1978).

Henley, Nancy, *Body Politics* (Englewood Cliffs NJ: Prentice-Hall, 1977).

Irigaray, Luce, 'This Sex Which Is Not One', in Marks and de Courtivron, *New French Feminisms*.

Kaplan, E. Ann, *Women and Film* (New York: Methuen, 1983).

Lacan, Jacques, *Écrits*, tr. Alan Sheridan (New York: W. W. Norton, 1972).

Marks, Elaine, and de Courtivron, Isabelle (eds), *New French Feminisms* (New York: Schocken, 1981).

Mulvey, Laura, 'Visual Pleasure and Narrative Cinema', *Screen*, 16.3 (1975).

Silverman, Kaja, *The Subject of Semiotics* (New York: Oxford University Press, 1983).

Index

Note: n = endnote; **bold** = extended discussion